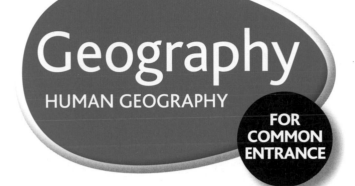

Geography

HUMAN GEOGRAPHY

FOR COMMON ENTRANCE

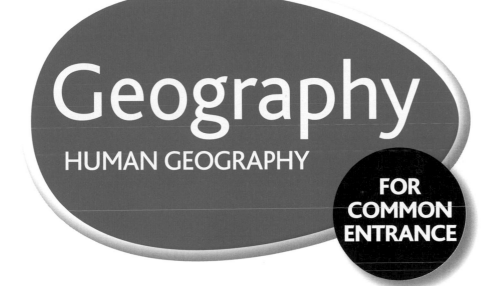

Geography

HUMAN GEOGRAPHY

FOR COMMON ENTRANCE

James Dale-Adcock

Series Editor: Simon Lewis

GALORE PARK

AN HACHETTE UK COMPANY

The Publishers would like to thank the following for permission to reproduce copyright material:

Photo credits p1 © dancurko / iStock / Thinkstock **p10 (t)** © Rafael Ben-Ari – Fotolia.com **p10 (b)** © pjhpix – Fotolia.com **p11 (t)** © ATGImages / iStock / Thinkstock **p11 (b)** © Robert Morris / Alamy **p 12** © jool-yan – Fotolia.com **p27 (t)** © Pavel Losevsky – Fotolia.com **p27 (bl)** © Jenifoto – Fotolia.com **p27 (br)** © AndyRowland / iStock/Thinkstock **p29 (t)** © Scott Thomas / iStock / Thinkstock **p29 (b)** © grafxart8888 / iStock / Thinkstock **p30 (t)** © Karen Kasmauski / Science Faction / Getty images **p30 (b)** © underwaterstas – Fotolia.com **p31 (t)** © PLANETOBSERVER / SCIENCE PHOTO LIBRARY **p31 (b)** © NOEL CELIS/AFP/ Getty Images **p33** © Mark Pearson / Alamy **p34** © economic images / Alamy **p36 (t)** © Purestock / Thinkstock **p36 (b)** © XiXinXing / iStock / Thinkstock **p42 (t)** © Pukkashots.com / Alamy **p42 (mt)** © Andrew Holt / Alamy **p42 (mb)** © Cotswolds Photo Library / Alamy **p42 (b)** © Ian Dagnall / Alamy **p 46 (l)** © David J. Green / Alamy **p46 (r)** © incamerastock / Alamy **p48** © Richard Bird / Geograph.co.uk via Wikipedia Commons (Attribution ShareAlik Licence 2.0 Generic - http://creativecommons.org/licenses/by-sa/2.0/deed.en) **p52 (tl)** © irisphoto1 – Fotolia.com **p52 (tr)** © Gergo Orban / iStock / Thinkstock **p52 (bl)** © geogphotos / Alamy **p52 (br)** © Archimage / Alamy **p55** © Neil Cooper / Alamy **p56** © Cifotart – Fotolia.com **p65** © starekase / iStock/Thinkstock **p66** © Robert Read Road Signs / Alamy **p67 (tl)** © Goinyk Volodymyr – Fotolia.com **p67 (tr)** © Remains / iStock / Thinkstock **p67 (cl)** © ivolodina – Fotolia.com **p67 (cr)** © samer chand / iStock / Thinkstock **p67 (b)** © kirstyokeeffe / iStock / Thinkstock **p68** © claudiodivizia / iStock / Thinkstock **p69 (t)** © dmitrydesigner – Fotolia.com **p69 (b)** © ValMansfield / iStock / Thinkstock **p70** © Kevin Clark / Alamy **p73** © steverts / iStock / Thinkstock **p75 (t)** © HERVE DONNEZAN / SCIENCE PHOTO LIBRARY **p75 (b)** © Hemeroskopion – Fotolia.com **p76 (l)** © kzenon / iStock / Thinkstock **p76 (r)** © luchshen – Fotolia.com **p79** © Jiri Rezac / Alamy **p82** © Image Source White / Image Source / Thinkstock **p84 (t)** © morenosoppelsa / iStock / Thinkstock **p84 (b)** © tim gartside london / Alamy **p85** © david martyn hughes / Alamy **p86 (t)** © Skyscan Photolibrary / Alamy **p86 (b)** © Paul Thompson Images / Alamy **p87** © Creatas / Thinkstock **p88** © Jon Arnold Images Ltd / Alamy **p89 (t)** © Photofusion Picture Library / Alamy **p89 (b)** © Jon Hicks / Alamy **p91** © Mark Boulton / Alamy **p92** © Photo Japan / Alamy **p93** © David Jones / PA Archive / Press Association Images **p94** © Anwar Hussain / Demotix / Demotix / Press Association Images **p95** © STRDEL/AFP/ Getty Images **p97** © SCPhotos / Alamy **p100** © mur162 – Fotolia.com **p102** © Bernard Breton / iStock / Thinkstock **p104** © septemberlegs / iStock / Thinkstock **p105** © David Poole / Alamy **p106** © Chris Howes / Wild Places Photography / Alamy **p109** © PHILIPPE PLAILLY / SCIENCE PHOTO LIBRARY **p110** © Gavin Hellier / Alamy **p115** © G P Bowater / Alamy **p116** © gnomeandi / iStockEditorial / Thinkstock **p117 (t)** © Sergio Boccardo / iStock/Thinkstock **p117 (b)** © First Hydro Company – which is part of a joint venture between International Power Ltd. and Mitsui & Co., Ltd **p118** © First Hydro Company – which is part of a joint venture between International Power Ltd. and Mitsui & Co., Ltd **p122** © Stocktrek Images / Thinkstock **p141** © Cultura Creative (RF) / Alamy

Acknowledgements This product includes mapping data licensed from Ordnance Survey® reproduced by permission of Ordnance Survey on behalf of HMSO. © Crown copyright 2007. All rights reserved. Ordnance Survey Licence number 150001477. Ordnance Survey and the OS symbol are registered trademarks and Explorer and Landranger are trademarks of the Ordnance Survey, the national mapping agency of Great Britain.

Every effort has been made to trace all copyright holders, but if any have been inadvertently overlooked the Publishers will be pleased to make the necessary arrangements at the first opportunity.

Although every effort has been made to ensure that website addresses are correct at time of going to press, Galore Park cannot be held responsible for the content of any website mentioned in this book. It is sometimes possible to find a relocated web page by typing in the address of the home page for a website in the URL window of your browser.

Hachette UK's policy is to use papers that are natural, renewable and recyclable products and made from wood grown in sustainable forests.

The logging and manufacturing processes are expected to conform to the environmental regulations of the country of origin.

Orders: please contact Bookpoint Ltd, 130 Milton Park, Abingdon, Oxon OX14 4SB. Telephone: +44 (0)1235 827827. Lines are open 9.00a.m.–5.00p.m., Monday to Saturday, with a 24-hour message answering service. Visit our website at www.galorepark.co.uk for details of other revision guides for Common Entrance, examination papers and Galore Park publications.

Published by Galore Park Publishing Ltd,

An Hachette UK company

Carmelite House, 50 Victoria Embankment, London EC4Y 0DZ

www.galorepark.co.uk

Text copyright © James Dale-Adcock 2014

The right of James Dale-Adcock to be identified as the author of this work has been asserted by him in accordance with sections 77 and 78 of the Copyright, Designs and Patents Act 1988.

Impression number   10 9 8 7 6 5 4 3

2018 2017

Typeset in 11.5/13 pt ITC Officina Book

Illustrations by Aptara, Inc.

Printed in India

A catalogue record for this title is available from the British Library
ISBN: 978 1 471827 28 0

About the author

James Dale-Adcock held the post of Head of Geography at Cranleigh Preparatory School for fifteen years and is currently their Director of Studies. During this time James has worked closely with Elizabeth Holtom (author of the successful *Study Skills*) to produce a range of resources which develop skills for pupils regardless of their learning style or level.

James also sits on the governing body at another local Surrey school and is actively involved in directing education policy at his own school and within the independent preparatory sector as a whole.

James has travelled extensively throughout Europe and beyond, a hobby that has fuelled his passion for geography and, when his young family is a little older, he wishes to return to – preferably on his motorbike!

Contents

Introduction

The target audience for this textbook is Year 7 and 8 pupils working towards the ISEB Common Entrance Geography exam. Having studied the physical processes which shape our landscape in *Geography for Common Entrance: Physical Geography*, this book now explores the impact humankind has had on the landscape and environment. Together, these books form a course which cements skills and subject material identified in both the recently revised National Curriculum syllabus and ISEB syllabus. Remember to look out for 'Exam tip' boxes which are useful for revision purposes. These concise text boxes provide insight into what an exam marker may be looking for in an answer.

Study of location knowledge is graduated over the two-book Geography for Common Entrance series. This book builds upon the foundation level location knowledge material found in *Geography for Common Entrance: Physical Geography*, adding a final layer of information and questions as required for the Common Entrance examination at the end of Year 8.

These extra passages are supported by appropriately more challenging extension questions.

Although modelled around the ISEB syllabus, both books in the series contain stand-alone chapters and sub-chapters which are not directly examined within the syllabus. These are included to help broaden the knowledge of all children, but particularly those working towards scholarship examinations.

Notes on features in this book

Each chapter is punctuated by keywords which are coloured blue. Definitions of these keywords can be found in the glossary at the end of the book. To assist with exam preparation those words in the glossary which are directly used in the Common Entrance syllabus are coloured blue and underlined. These syllabus words may be used in exam questions and would appear in the best answers written by pupils.

The recently revised ISEB Common Entrance and Common Academic Scholarship syllabus places a significant emphasis on learning theory and skills based on topic case studies and, where possible, contemporary examples. This approach permeates this textbook, with every opportunity taken to relate theory and skills to detailed recent examples. The reader is also given tailored guidance of how to research suitable contemporary examples through the 'Geography in the news' boxes.

Mapwork

Being able to interpret and use an Ordnance Survey (<u>OS</u>) map is one of the key skills you will need in order to do well in a Geography exam. By now you are probably a skilled user of OS maps at 1:25000 and 1:50000 scales. This chapter will help you remember and practise the skills you have already developed, and will introduce you to further skills, so that you will be able to answer any question relating to the OS map that comes with the Geography paper.

In this chapter you will study:

■ **Figure 1.1:** Using an Ordnance Survey map in the field to recognise features of the landscape

- using four-figure and six-figure grid references to identify features on a map
- determining the direction one map feature is from another and measuring the distance between map features
- recognising the height of places on a map and visualising what the landscape would look like if you were at ground level
- understanding which map symbols are commonly used and grouping features on the map into human and physical features.

In addition, this chapter will help you understand how OS maps can be used to answer questions about other topics in Geography.

◯ 1.1 Basic skills revision: grid references, distance and height on OS maps

Mapwork words used in exam questions

More than ever the OS map is being used in several sections of Geography exams. This means that you must be a skilled user of OS maps and must look out for the mapwork words used in questions relating to the map, highlighted in bold below.

You will definitely be asked questions concerning the location of map features using a <u>four-figure grid reference</u> or a **six-figure grid reference**. If you do not know the map symbol that appears at the grid reference given, look at the <u>key</u>, or legend, which is a list of all the different symbols on the map and the meaning of these symbols (see Appendix, pages 156–159). Have a look at these now.

OS maps are divided up into even squares, called **grid squares**. Whatever the **scale** of the OS map, the area of land covered within 1 grid square is always $1\,km^2$. Grid squares are created by the vertical and horizontal thin blue lines on the map (see Figure 1.2). The vertical thin blue lines are called <u>eastings</u> because the numbers increase in value as you go east. The horizontal thin blue lines are called <u>northings</u> because the numbers increase in value as you go north. Each easting and northing is given a two digit number to be identified by and this number can be found at either end of the line.

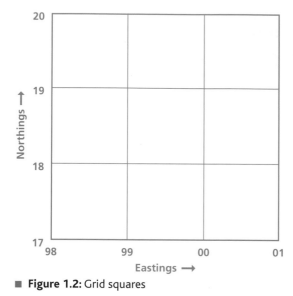

■ **Figure 1.2:** Grid squares

Often a mapwork question will ask candidates to describe an aspect of the map (such as the <u>relief</u>) above or below a northing, or to one side of an easting. If you are asked to describe the relief of any given area of the map, you should describe the height of the land. You will need to use <u>contour lines</u> and **spot heights** to identify the exact height and shape of the land. Here is an example which refers to the map of Arundel on page 23:

Question: Describe the relief of the land to the north of northing 07

You might already have the mapwork skills to answer this question; if in doubt, read through the rest of this revision chapter to help you.

Using four-figure grid references

In most exams you will, at least once, have to give or interpret a four-figure grid reference. Four-figure grid references allow you to identify a specific grid square using the numbers at either end of the eastings and northings.

Here is a reminder of what to do when you want to tell somebody where something is on a map. Remember the bottom left hand corner is the meeting point of easting and northing, whether you are giving or receiving a four-figure grid reference. Use the saying 'go along the corridor before you go up the stairs' to remind yourself to always give the easting reference first, followed by the northing reference.

Look at Figure 1.3. Identify which grid square *Perry Hill* is in.

Step 1: Find *Perry Hill* which is to the north east of *Burpham*.

Step 2: Go to the bottom left hand corner of the grid square that contains *Perry Hill*.

Step 3: Start by finding the easting reference. Follow the easting (the vertical line) from this point to the end of the line (either at the top or bottom) where you will find its two-digit identity number. Write down this number: 05.

Step 4: Now find the northing reference. Return to the bottom left hand corner of the grid square containing Perry Hill. Follow the northing (the horizontal line) from this point to the end of the line where you will find its two-digit identity number. Write down this number: 09.

Step 5: You should now have a four-digit number – 0509 – which is the four-figure grid reference for the grid square containing *Perry Hill*. Remember to write down the easting reference first, followed by the northing reference.

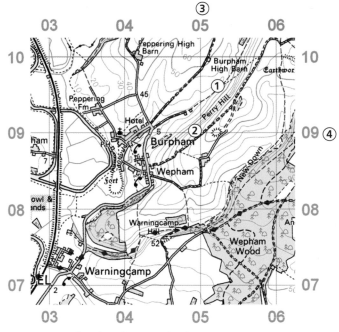

■ **Fig. 1.3:** Finding four-figure grid reference

Here is a reminder of what to do when you are given a grid reference.

Look at Figure 1.4. The grid square you need to find is 0307.

Step 1: Split the grid reference 0307 into two parts: 03 and 07.

Step 2: The first two-digit number always refers to the easting. Find easting 03 and put one finger of your right hand on it.

Step 3: The second two-digit number always refers to the northing. Find northing 07 and put one finger of your left hand on it.

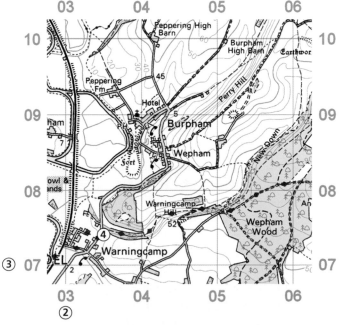

■ **Figure 1.4:** Finding a grid square based on a four-figure reference

Step 4: Move both of your fingers along the grid lines until they meet. This is the bottom left hand corner of the grid square you need to find: 0307.

Using six-figure grid references

We use six–figure grid references to pinpoint exactly where a given feature is within a grid square. This more accurate grid reference is created by imagining nine extra eastings and nine extra northings within the grid square. This gives you an extra digit to the two-digit easting and two-digit northing numbers. When they are put together, they create a six-figure grid reference. Don't forget to continue to obey the bottom left hand corner rule, which you can remember with the saying 'go along the corridor before you go up the stairs'.

Here is a reminder of what to do when you want to tell someone exactly where something is on a map.

Look at Figure 1.5. You want to identify precisely where the *public house* is to the north-west of *Wepham*.

Step 1: Find the *PH (public house)* to the north-west of *Wepham*.

Step 2: Using Figure 1.4, Identify the four-figure grid reference for the grid square that the *PH* is in. Your answer should read 0308. If it does not, check again how to do four-figure grid references.

Step 3: To find the two extra digits, go to the bottom left hand corner of grid square 0308. For the extra easting digit, imagine nine extra eastings running vertically across the square. These are not normally drawn on maps but are shown in Figure 1.5 to help you. How many lines across do you have to go before reaching the *PH*? Write this single-digit number after the first part of the four-figure grid reference (03_). You should have 038.

Step 4: To find the extra northing digit, return to the bottom left hand corner of the grid square containing the *PH*. This time, imagine nine extra northings running horizontally up the square. How many lines up do you have to go before reaching the *PH*? Write this single-digit number after the second part of the four-figure grid reference (08_). You should have 088.

■ **Figure 1.5:** Finding a six-figure grid reference

Step 5: Put the two sets of numbers together, eastings first and then northings. You now have a six-figure grid reference for the *PH* to the north-west of *Wepham* which should read 038088.

Here is a reminder of what to do when you are given a six-figure grid reference.

Look at Figure 1.6 which shows grid square 0509 in the centre. Use the following steps to identify the feature at grid reference 051099.

Step 1: Divide the grid reference 051099 into two parts (051 and 099) and underline the first two digits of each set of numbers to find the four-figure grid reference first (051 and 099 tell us that the four-figure grid reference is 0509).

■ **Figure 1.6:** Finding a feature based on a six-figure reference

Step 2: Find the four-figure grid reference and put one finger of your right hand and one finger of your left hand on the bottom left hand corner of this grid square.

Step 3: Look again at the first set of numbers: 051. The third digit, the one you have not underlined, tells you how many imaginary extra eastings you need to move across the grid square. Imagine nine extra eastings running across the square and move the finger of your right hand across the grid square to imaginary easting 1. These imaginary eastings are not normally drawn on maps but are in Figure 1.6 to help you. Keep your finger on this point.

Step 4: Look again at the second set of numbers 099. The third digit, the one you have not underlined, tells you how many imaginary extra northings you need to move up the grid square. Imagine nine extra northings running up the square and move the finger of your left hand up the grid square to imaginary northing 9. These imaginary northings are not normally drawn on maps but are shown in Figure 1.6 to help you.

Step 5: Now move your right finger vertically and your left finger horizontally along these imaginary grid lines until they meet. Your fingers should meet at *Burpham High Barn*.

Identifying direction on OS maps

Remember never to use the words *above*, *below*, *left* or *right* when answering a mapwork question about direction. Instead, use the directions of the eight-point <u>compass</u> (Figure 1.7) north, south,

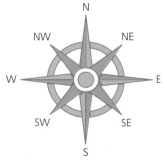

■ **Figure 1.7:** The eight-point compass

east and west. You may want to use the rhyme 'never eat shredded wheat' to help you remember this.

Here is an example. Look at Figure 1.3 (page 3). You would say that the fort at grid reference 038084 is to the *west* of Wepham, *not* to the *left* of Wepham. Remember, when giving the direction of something that lies between the north, south, east and west points, we always say north and south first, *not* east and west (for example, north-east *not* east-north; south-west *not* west-south).

Giving and receiving directions is easy but you must remember to always read the question carefully. Look at the two questions below which refer to Figure 1.3 (on page 3). They look like the same question, but the words in italic, *to* and *from,* mean that the correct answers are in fact opposite to each other.

Question 1: Which direction is it from Burpham *to* Perry Hill?	Question 2: Which direction is Burpham *from* Perry Hill?
Answer 1: north-east	Answer 2: south-west

For precise directions, the eight-point compass is broken down into the 360 degrees of a circle which we call **bearings**. North has a value of 0° or 360°, east is at 90°, south is at 180° and west is at 270°. To give a bearing as a direction, place your protractor on the map with 0° or 360° facing straight up in a northerly direction, making sure your protractor remains parallel to the eastings. Then, with your protractor fixed in place, use a ruler to line up the features in the question with the centre of your protractor and read the correct bearing off the protractor.

Look at Figure 1.8. Place the centre of your protractor on the *church* in *Burpham* at grid reference 039090. Remember to place your protractor on the map with the 0° facing straight up in a northerly direction. Find the bearing from the *church* to *Burpham High Barn* at grid reference 051099. You should have a bearing of 50°.

Measuring distance and area on OS maps

The OS maps you use in exams have scale ratios of either 1:25 000 or 1:50 000, meaning distances on these maps are 25 000 or 50 000 times bigger in real life. You will have already practised your mapwork skills on maps of these scales, but to remind yourself look at the 1:25 000 map of Seaford on page 24 and the 1:50 000 map of Arundel on page 23. Remember that although similar features can be found on both types of maps they have different keys with different symbols. The Appendix shows the key from a 1:50 000 scale map (pages 158–159) and the key from a 1:25 000 scale map (pages 156–157). The grid lines on OS maps do not change with the scale; a grid square on any OS map at any scale

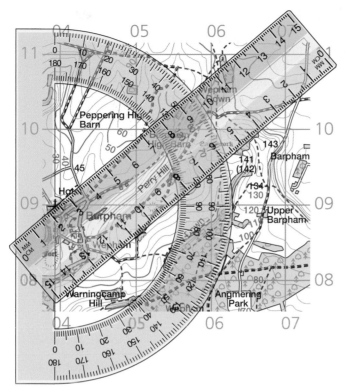

■ **Figure 1.8:** Finding a bearing

is always 1 km². You can see what scale a map is by looking at the **scale ratio**, which can always be found at the bottom of the map.

Below the scale ratio you will find the **scale bar** which helps you convert any distances you measure on the map from centimetres to kilometres (you will need a ruler). Ignore the scale measuring miles; we do not use this. On 1:50 000 scale maps, one centimetre is equal to half a kilometre (500 metres). On 1:25 000 scale maps, one centimetre is equal to a quarter of a kilometre (250 metres). Therefore, when measuring distances in a straight line, or 'as the crow flies', you simply lay your ruler on the map, line up the two points you have been asked to measure the distance between and take a measurement on your ruler. A simple calculation using the scale bar will give you the answer.

For a measured distance taken from a 1:50 000 map you need to divide centimetres by 2 to get kilometres.

For example: measured distance on map 10 cm
actual distance is 10 cm ÷ 2 = 5 km

For a measured distance taken from a 1:25 000 map you need to divide centimetres by 4 to get kilometres.

For example: measured distance on map 12 cm
              actual distance is 12 cm ÷ 4 = 3 km

However, you may be asked to measure the distance between two places along a winding route. In this case a ruler will not give you an accurate answer, so you should use a piece of paper or a piece of string to measure the distance along the route, marking points on the edge of the paper, and then place it next to your ruler to get an answer in centimetres.

For example: look at the 1:50 000 map extract of Arundel on page 23. Measure the distance along the railway track between the stations at the following grid references: 001042 and 026118. You should measure approximately 20 cm which you divide by 2, as this is a 1:50 000 scale map, giving you a measurement of 2 km.

Sometimes you may be asked to work out, or estimate, the size of a particular area on a map.
    To do this, you need to remember the following:

- on 1:50 000 maps, 1 cm² is equal to 0.25 km² $\left(\frac{1}{4}\,\text{km}^2\right)$

- on 1:25 000 maps, 1 cm² is equal to 0.0625 km² $\left(\frac{1}{16}\,\text{km}^2\right)$

So, to calculate the size of a particular area in km²:

- on 1:50 000 maps, divide the number of 1 cm² by 4
- on 1:25 000 maps, divide the number of 1 cm² by 16

With this information at hand it is easy to work out the area of square or rectangular shaped areas on the map. However, the landscape is rarely so even. Therefore it is more than likely you will have to estimate, with the help of your ruler, how many square centimetres an irregular shaped area covers, before making your conversion to kilometres. Here is an example, this time using a map at 1:25 000 scale:
    Look at the 1:25 000 map extract of Seaford in Figure 1.9.

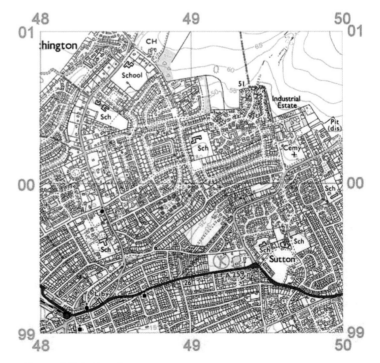

■ **Figure 1.9**: Estimating an area

Estimate the area covered by buildings in Seaford to the north of the A259 but no further west than easting 48. You do this by imagining each grid square divided into $16 \times 1\,cm^2$. You then look at each grid square in the area specified and work out as carefully as you can roughly how many $1\,cm^2$ are covered in housing. For example, grid square 4900 has about $8 \times 1\,cm^2$ covered in housing north of the A259; 4899 has about $12 \times 1\,cm^2$ of housing. Do this for all the grid squares and then calculate how many $1\,km^2$ you have in total. You should have around $49 \times 1\,cm^2$.

We know that $1\,cm^2$ on a 1:25 000 map is equivalent to $\frac{1}{16}\,km^2$, so divide 49 by 16 to give an answer of around $3\,km^2$.

Recognising spot heights, triangulation pillars and contour lines

The height and shape, or relief, of the land is represented in two ways on OS maps. Remember, all heights are given in metres above sea level. Firstly, spot heights are used to give the exact height at a particular point on a map and can be identified by a very small black dot, often but not always on or near a road, with a number written in black ink next to the dot. Look at Figure 1.3 (page 3) at grid reference 042095 and you will see a spot height reading 45 metres above sea level. If a spot height is the highest point in that area of the map it will be surrounded by a blue triangle called a **triangulation pillar**. There may be more than one triangulation pillar on an OS map extract but they will not be located close to each other. Look at the map extract of Arundel on page 23 and you will find, if you look very carefully, four triangulation pillars spread across the map. For example, there is one at 998082.

The second method of representing relief on OS maps is by means of contour lines. These thin brown lines join areas of equal height. On 1:50 000 scale maps a height change of 10 metres divides each contour line whereas on 1:25 000 scale maps a height change of 5 metres divides each contour line. Whether you are using a 1:50 000 or 1:25 000 scale map, remember that when the contour lines are close together a steep **gradient** is being represented and when they are spread further apart it indicates a more gentle relief.

Look at the map of Arundel on page 23. Compare the contour lines in grid square 0505 to the contour lines in grid square 0810 and you should immediately see that the relief is much steeper in grid square 0810 as the contour lines are packed much closer together. Note that the 100 metre contour line in grid square 0810 is thicker than the others around it. This is because on 1:50 000 scale maps the contour lines at every 50 metres are thicker than the others and on 1:25 000 scale maps the contour lines are thicker at 25 metre intervals.

Using contour lines to visualise relief and draw sketch sections

Steep slope

■ **Figure 1.10:** Steep slope

Gentle slope

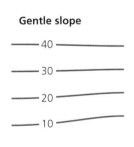

■ **Figure 1.11:** Gentle slope

Round top hill

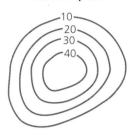

■ **Figure 1.12:** Round top hill

Flat top hill

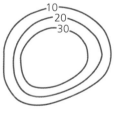

■ **Figure 1.13:** Flat top hill

Valley

10
20
30
40

■ **Figure 1.14:** Valley

Contour lines, and the patterns they create, allow you not only to evaluate the height of the land but also to visualise the shape of the land. It is a very useful skill to be able to recognise contour line patterns which identify **relief features** such as round top hills, flat top hills, valleys and ridges.

Round top hills (Figure 1.12) are shown by circular contour lines within each other increasing in height steadily towards the peak of the hill or mountain. Flat top hills (Figure 1.13) are similar to round top hills except the contour lines become much more spread out or disappear towards the centre of the circular shape. This is because after an initial increase in gradient the hill flattens at the top, forming a **plateau** or a **ridge**. Valleys (Figure 1.14) are illustrated on maps by a 'V' shape pattern of contour lines pointing towards the top of the valley or source of any stream or river flowing in the valley. Can you find examples of any of the relief features shown in Figures 1.10–14 on the map of Arundel on page 23?

If you can visualise the relief by interpreting the contour lines on a map then you will have no problem in drawing a simple **sketch section** of what you would see from a given point on the map. You are most likely to be asked to draw a sketch section along a northing and between two eastings within a grid square. This means you will need to locate the grid square on the map and then use the contour lines to sketch out the relief of the land as you would see it along the northing. Depending on how many marks there are awarded for the question you might need to add features such as buildings, roads or woodland to your sketch by interpreting map symbols.

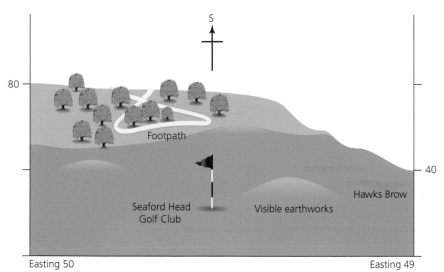

Footpath

Seaford Head
Golf Club

Visible earthworks

Hawks Brow

80

40

S

Easting 50

Easting 49

■ **Figure 1.15:** Drawing a sketch section

Look at the map extract of Seaford on page 24. You are standing on the golf course at grid reference 494983 facing south. Draw a sketch section view of what you would see between easting 49 and easting 50; remember you are facing south! Your sketch should show a ridge rising from 40 to 80 metres with a copse in the eastern section, through which a crossing path runs. You may also include the visible earthworks close to where you are standing in the west (see Figure 1.15).

> **→ Exam tip**
>
> Even if you are under time pressure, try not to rush when working with grid references as it only creates mistakes. If you are given a six-figure grid reference you will usually find that the answer is a map feature that cannot be confused with something nearby. Always use the eight points of the compass to indicate direction and be careful to read the question concerning direction carefully; the words *to* and *from* can easily be confused. Remember that spot heights are very small and are sometimes almost hidden by the other information on the map. With contour lines you may need to trace your way round to the point where the height is written or count the number of lines up or down to find the value of the contour line you are looking at.

Exercise 1A

All questions refer either to the map extract of Arundel on page 23 or to the map extract of Seaford on page 24. You may need to refer to the keys (pages 156–159) to find the answers to these questions.

1   Name a feature you can find on the map of Arundel in the following grid squares:

 (a) 0704   (c) 0610

 (b) 0109   (d) 0004

2 (a) There are eleven schools on the map of Seaford. Give the six-figure grid reference for five of them.

 (b) For the five you have chosen, list which direction each school lies from the leisure centre at grid reference 493994.

3   What job would you do if you worked in Seaford at the following grid references:

 (a) 481991   (c) 506995

 (b) 494982   (d) 485985

4 (a) How far is it 'as the crow flies' from Whiteways Lodge on the Arundel map at grid reference 003107 to the Public House (PH) just to the west of Hammerpot at grid reference 066057?

 (b) How far would it be if you measured this distance along the road taking the A284 followed by the A27?

5   Describe the relief of Arundel Park which can be found to the north-west of Arundel.

Extension questions

All questions refer either to the map extract of Arundel on page 23 or to the map extract of Seaford on page 24. You may need to refer to the keys (pages 156–159) to find the answers to these questions.

6   Give the six-figure grid references and heights of all four triangulation pillars that appear on the Arundel map extract.

7   Identify the relief features at the following grid references on the Arundel map extract:

 (a) 017087   (c) 081101

 (b) 070090   (d) 995077

8   Estimate the area covered by sea on the map extract of Seaford (page 24).

9   Using the map of Arundel (page 23), compare the relief in the north-east of this map extract to the relief in the south-west of the extract.

10 You are standing facing east at grid reference 470006 on the Seaford map. Draw a sketch section of what you would see between northing 003 and northing 008.

1 Mapwork

14

1.2 Map symbols showing human and physical features

Common map symbols – syllabus extra/scholarship

Geography exams require you to answer a lot of questions in a short period, so it is useful to find ways of saving time.

To save time in the mapwork section of an exam it is useful to learn the common map symbols that you may well be asked to identify. Learning some of these symbols will save you valuable minutes as you won't have to turn the map over to identify the symbol on the key.

Symbol	Meaning	Key category
	Viewpoint	Tourist and leisure
	Information centre (all year/seasonal)	Tourist and leisure
	Country park	Tourist and leisure
	Nature reserve	Tourist and leisure
	Off road cycle routes	Other public access
	National Trail/Recreational route	Other public access
	Places of worship (churches)	General features
	Youth hostel	General features
	Orchard	Vegetation
	Marsh, reeds or saltings	Vegetation

■ **Figure 1.16:** Selected map symbols from 1:25 000 maps

There are particular map symbols for 1:25 000 maps and 1:50 000 maps – see the Appendix on pages 156–159. Try to familiarise yourself with as many of the symbols as you can from these keys. Figures 1.16 and 1.17 provide a useful selection of symbols from each.

Symbol	Meaning	Key category
P P&R / P&R	Parking, Park and ride, all year/seasonal	Tourist information
⚑	Golf course or links	Tourist information
 ☏ ☏	Telephone, public/motoring organisation	Tourist information
 ⛺ 🚐	Camp site/Caravan site	Tourist information
P	Post office	Abbreviations
PH	Public house	Abbreviations
	National Park	Boundaries
 ⬛	National Trust – always open	Land features
---------------	Footpath	Public rights of way
— — — — — — —	Bridleway	Public rights of way

■ **Figure 1.17:** Selected map symbols from 1:50 000 maps

Identifying human and physical features

Features on maps are split into two different groups. **Physical features** are those things on the map that are clearly natural, such as an area of wild woodland, a river, the sea or hills and valleys. Any feature on the map that is in some way man-made is called a human feature, for example roads, schools, railway lines and stations. Whether identifying human or physical features, always try to refer to something specific rather than giving a general answer. Look at Figure 1.18 (page 17). In grid square 0978 we can identify several specific physical features such as valleys, streams and a steep hillside. Check you can identify each one of these correctly. Use the 1:50 000 scale in the Appendix to remind you. In grid square 0876 we can identify several **human features** such as the paper mill, a pier, the railway line and the A830 main road.

It is important to make sure you do not give ambiguous answers when asked to identify physical or human features on a map. Do not choose a feature that could be physical or human. Here is an example. Look at Figure 1.18 (page 17). The coniferous woodland in the north west section of the map could be interpreted as a physical or human feature as this type of woodland is usually a man-made plantation. Other features that could be ambiguous include man-made lakes or reservoirs and canals.

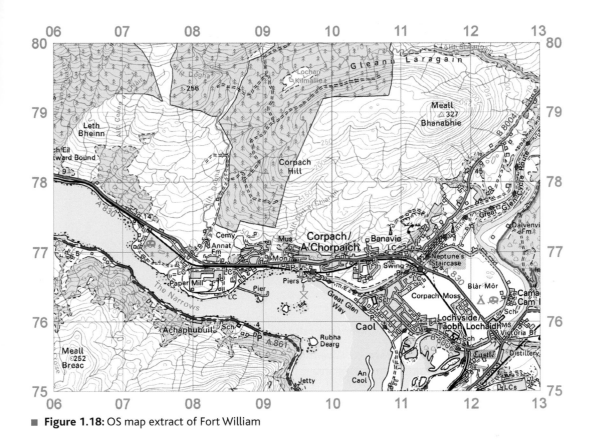

■ **Figure 1.18:** OS map extract of Fort William

Describing routes

A good knowledge of map symbols and their meanings is useful when a question asks you to describe a route across an OS map. The examiner will be looking for accuracy in your description and will allocate marks for identification of physical and human features along the journey. You should also make reference to the altitude. The route may be a short walk of a few kilometres along a footpath on the map or may be a longer journey following a road or railway and you should identify the distance travelled.

Look at the map extract from the Peak District on page 26. Imagine you were asked to describe what you would see from a boat travelling down the River Noe from where the river enters the map in grid square 1783 to where it leaves the map in grid square 1882. Physical features you would see include the flat valley floor (**floodplain**), woodland and river meanders. Human features you would pass include bridges, a sewage works, a mill and a caravan/campsite. Do not forget to use the directions of the eight-point compass rather than using the words up, down, left and right, and give precise grid references where possible (for example, the mill on the north bank of the river at grid reference 173837).

> **Exam tip**
>
> Remember to go for obviously man-made structures when asked to identify a human feature on the map, such as a specific building like a school, church or post office. If it is a physical feature you are looking for, remember the different relief features that contour lines represent. Whether it is a human or physical feature you are asked for, make sure you don't give an ambiguous answer.

Exercise 1B

Questions 1 and 2 refer to the 1:50 000 map extract of the Isle of Wight on page 25. Questions 3 and 4 refer to the 1:25 000 map extract of the Peak District on page 26.

1 Look at the Isle of Wight map on page 25. What is the meaning of the map symbols at the following grid references?

(a) 547777   (b) 548797   (c) 533782

2 Give the four-figure grid reference of any caravan/campsite on the map.

3 Look at the map of the Peak District on page 26. Give three pieces of map evidence that suggest tourism is important in this area.

4 Follow the A6187 from the car park in Castleton (149832) to the campsite north-east of Brough (186828). Describe two physical and two human features you would see out of the window if you were making this journey in a car.

Extension questions

5 Using the Isle of Wight map extract on page 25, identify with a six-figure grid reference one example of each of the 1:50 000 symbols listed in Figure 1.17. (page 16), with the exception of a National Park.

6 Look at the map extract from the Peak District on page 26. Describe the fastest route on foot between Bradwell 1781 and Castleton 1582. Refer to physical and human features you would pass on your journey.

◯ 1.3 How OS maps can be used to study other topics

Geography exams may require that you use your map skills throughout the paper. After you have completed the Mapwork section of the exam, don't be tempted to fold up the OS map and think you can get on with the rest of the paper without using it. The map can sometimes be used in relation to questions in other sections of the paper, so leave it out on your desk.

Weathering, erosion, rivers and coasts

Most OS maps have either a river or a section of coastline on them so it is likely that a question regarding rivers or coasts will refer to the map. The questions could ask you about the formation of lowland or upland river features such as V-shaped valleys, waterfalls, meanders and ox-bow lakes or how coastal features such as headlands, bays and spits are created. The question could examine your knowledge of three types of weathering (physical or mechanical weathering, freeze-thaw and onion skin, biological and chemical weathering; these are discussed further in *Geography for Common Entrance: Physical Geography*, in Chapter 4: Landform processes) by asking you which process is likely to occur at a given point on the map and why. Your understanding of drainage may be tested by a question asking you to describe or analyse the drainage on the map provided.

Weather and climate

Within the topic of weather and climate, only the subject of microclimate is likely to be related to the OS map you are provided with. You may be asked to discuss the influences in a specific location on the OS map of human and physical features such as buildings, woodland, lakes, etc. on temperature and rainfall readings. You may need to consider how relief, indicated by the contour lines on the map, may also affect local temperature and precipitation readings due to the height of the land and also its aspect.

Transport and industry

As a 'human geography' topic, transport and industry can also be easily related to the OS map you have with your exam paper. You may be asked to identify a primary, secondary or tertiary industry from the map.

- Farms or woodland plantations that might be used for forestry are examples of **primary industry**.
- Industrial estates or 'works' indicate **secondary industry**.
- Schools, hospitals, hotels, shopping centres, tourist information centres and museums are all examples of **tertiary industry**.

Tourism

Quite often you will find that the OS map extract you have with your exam paper covers an area that is popular with tourists. The reason for this is that tourists are usually attracted to areas of natural beauty and such areas contain a variety of geographical features that you could be tested on in an exam. This is why it is particularly important to have a good knowledge of tourist-related map symbols.

   Tourism puts pressure on the **environment** and may conflict with the environment. For example, tourists walking off pathways in **National Parks** may cause **soil erosion**, damaging the very environment they have come to enjoy. **Settlement** growth, **urban**

sprawl, and the demand for new houses is another example of how the environment may be damaged as a result of a pressure placed upon it.

Population and settlement

Your knowledge of the <u>site</u>, <u>situation</u> and shape of settlements will be tested in the mapwork section of the CE paper. The next chapter explains how in more detail.

> **→ Exam tip**
>
> After you have completed the questions in the mapwork section of the exam, leave your OS map open on your desk. At some point you may have to refer back to the OS map in order to answer other questions. When asked to find map evidence, always give a four- or six-figure grid reference to show the examiner where the evidence exists.

Exercise 1C

Look at Figure 1.19 (on page 21), taken from a map extract of Exeter.

1 Look at the River Clyst in grid squares 9689 and 9789. What will happen to this section of the river in the future?

2 What is the name of the flat land that is either side of the River Clyst? Why are there no buildings on this land, and what do you think it will be used for? Give reasons for your answer.

3 What do you think would be the difference in night-time temperatures taken in grid squares 9392 and 9789? Explain your answer.

4 The school in grid square 9490 is built on the south-facing slope of Pyne's Hill. What effect is this going to have on temperature readings at the school and what else could influence how warm or cold it is at a school?

5 A supermarket covering 100 m^2 is to be built in or near Exeter. Give the six-figure grid reference of the site you would choose and three reasons for your choice.

6 Describe the drainage to the east of easting 97.

Extension questions

Look at the map extract of the Isle of Wight on page 25 for questions 7–9, 11 and 12, and the map extract of the Peak District on page 26 for question 10.

7 In grid square 5882 groynes enter the sea. Describe the process groynes are designed to stop.

8 Describe the types of coastal erosion that might have created Luccombe Bay and Horse Ledge in grid squares 5879 and 5880.

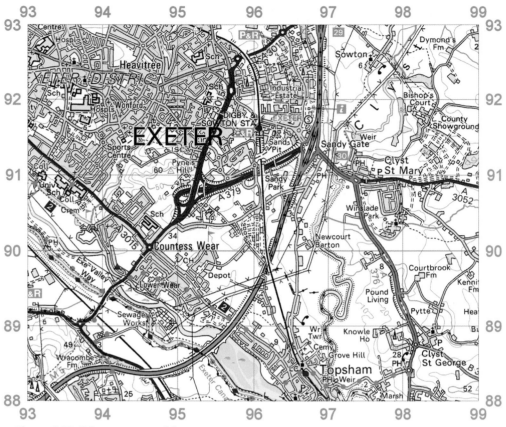

■ **Figure 1.19:** OS map extract of Exeter

9 What type of weathering do you think would occur on Shanklin Down 567801? Describe the stages of this process (you may find it useful to refer to *Geography for Common Entrance: Physical Geography,* Chapter 4: Landform processes).

10 If you were going to build a weather station within 1 km of Castleton, where would you put it and why?

11 Find and give the four-figure grid reference of an example of a primary industry and a tertiary industry on the map extract of the Isle of Wight.

12 (You may find it useful to refer to Chapter 2: Population and settlement for this question.)

 (a) What settlement pattern are Shanklin and Ventnor on the Isle of Wight map?

 (b) Why are they this settlement pattern?

 (c) List examples, with their four-figure grid references, of settlements on the Isle of Wight map that have different settlement patterns from Shanklin and Ventnor.

13 What evidence is there that different industries are placing pressure on the environment? Make reference to examples in both maps.

Exercise 1D: Enquiry suggestion

Use all the map skills you have acquired in this section to make a map of your school grounds or even part of your local town or village. Your teacher will direct you to the focus of your task. To help you with analysing what human and physical features are in the given area, you may want to refer to satellite imagery of your chosen area and satellite generated maps which can be found on websites such as www.bing.com and www.google.com. To work out the height of the land in order to add spot heights or contour lines to your map your teacher may provide you with suitable measuring equipment such as ranging poles and clinometers.

Exercise 1E: Past exam questions

Look at the OS map of the Peak District on page 26.

1 What do you find at 149828 and 153810? (2 marks)

2 In which direction does the River Noe flow? What map evidence shows this? (3 marks)

3 What is the distance by road from the junction at Goosehill (144828) to the church at Hope (172835)? Remember to answer in kilometres. (2 marks)

4 Give evidence to show how there have been changes in land use west of easting 16. (2 marks)

Exercise 1F

1 Solve the following clues.

(a) A geographer who makes maps (12 letters)

(b) ... pillar. Spot height surrounded by a blue triangle indicating the highest point in that area on the map (13 letters)

(c) A list of all the symbols used on a map and their meanings (3 letters)

(d) A flat topped area of high land (7 letters)

(e) Direction split up into 360° (8 letters)

(f) The shape and height of the land (6 letters)

(g) Term used to describe the steepness of a slope (8 letters)

(h) A black dot on an OS map with a number giving its height above sea level in metres (4 letters + 6 letters)

(i) A blue grid line running up and down an OS map (7 letters)

2 Make a list of all the key terms in this chapter and their definitions. Check your definitions against the glossary on page 160.

■ **Figure 1.20:** OS map extract of Arundel

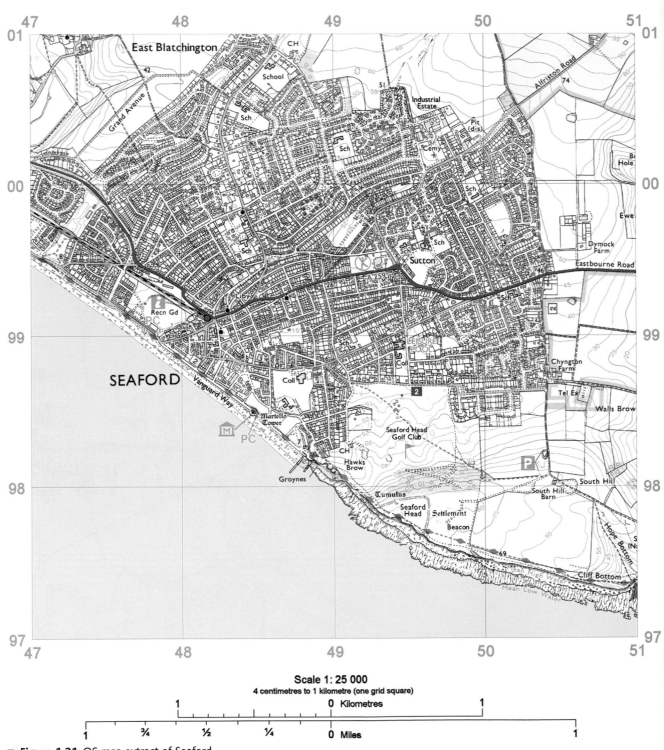

Scale 1: 25 000
4 centimetres to 1 kilometre (one grid square)

■ **Figure 1.21:** OS map extract of Seaford

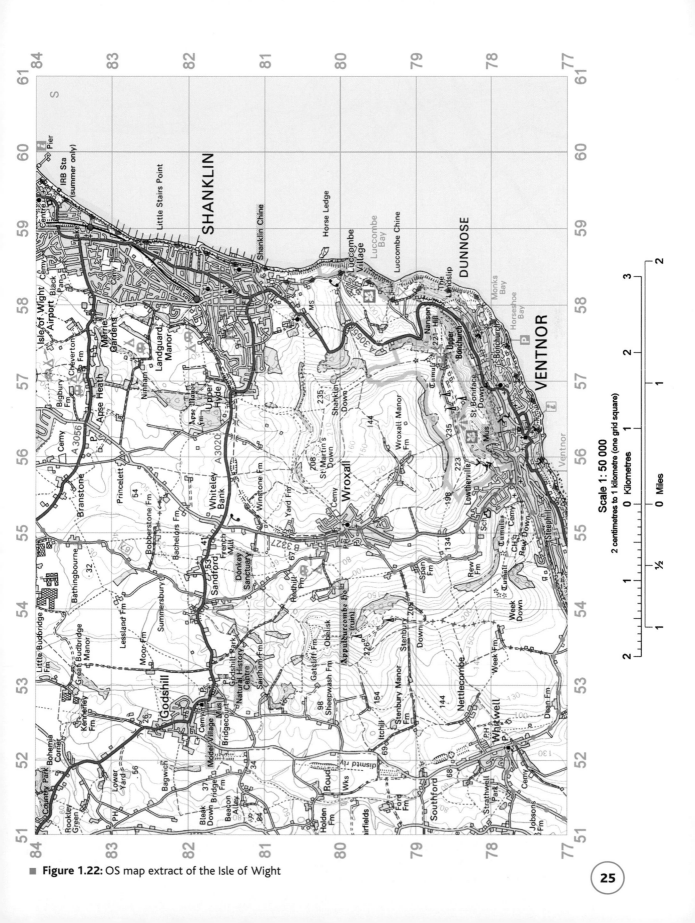

■ **Figure 1.22:** OS map extract of the Isle of Wight

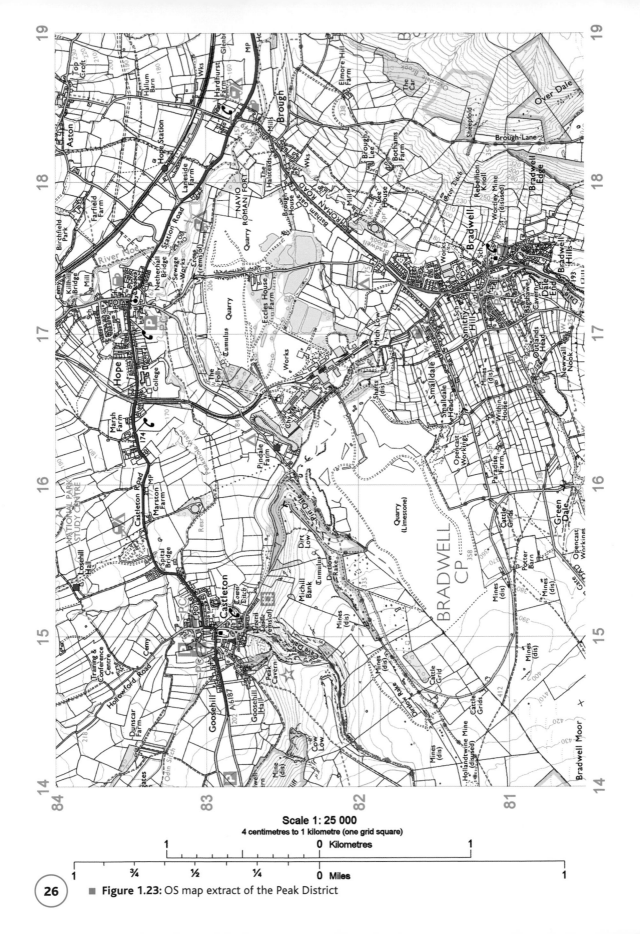

■ **Figure 1.23:** OS map extract of the Peak District

Scale 1: 25 000

4 centimetres to 1 kilometre (one grid square)

2 Population and settlement

A settlement is a place where people live. These places vary in size from tiny hamlets, where there may only be a few houses and no services, to megacities where the population may exceed 10 million people. Population is the total number of people living in a settlement. Of course a country's population is not evenly spread across its land, and the world's population is not evenly distributed either; people are concentrated in certain places for particular reasons.

In this chapter you will study:

■ **Figure 2.1:** A typical London street scene

- where people live in Britain and the rest of the world and why
- what causes changes in population levels and why the world's population is now over 7 billion
- why people first decided to live in a fixed place
- what factors they had to consider when choosing a place for a settlement
- how the shape of settlements changes over time
- the causes and effects of different types of migration.

■ **Figure 2.2:** A British town scene

■ **Figure 2.3:** A view of a UK village

27

2.1 Population distribution and changes in Britain and beyond

Are you in the middle of a crowd or surrounded by space?

Some people love to live right in the heart of a big bustling city. Others prefer wild open spaces. Of course people often have little choice of whether they live in urban or rural areas. If there are many people living in a place close together we call it **densely populated**. If there are fewer people spread over a place we would describe the area as **sparsely populated**.

Figure 2.4 shows how the population of the United Kingdom is spread or distributed. You will notice areas in the UK which are sparsely populated (0–10 people per square kilometre) are mountainous or upland areas, such as the Pennines, Scottish Highlands and Grampians, Snowdonia and Cambrian mountains in Wales and Dartmoor in the south-west of England. When early settlers chose places to build settlements these areas were not favoured, as soils were thin on the steep slopes and weather conditions were often harsh.

The population remains sparse in these areas today because steep slopes still limit accessibility, make building houses or industrial buildings challenging, and any farming that does take place tends to be **pastoral farming**, where sheep are left to graze over vast areas on the grass of mountain slopes. Many of these upland rural areas will now always remain sparsely populated as the government have designated them National Parks, such as Snowdonia National Park and The Lake District National Park. The building of new buildings, including homes, is severely restricted in national parks in order to maintain their rural beauty.

Now have a look at the areas on Figure 2.4 which are shaded in blue (over 150 people per kilometre). These densely populated areas are of course our cities, including London, Manchester, Birmingham, Leeds and Cardiff. Northern cities such as Leeds and Manchester began as trading settlements for the wool that came from sheep grazing on the Pennines, and later grew into important regional cities during the **Industrial Revolution**. Population levels have remained high in these areas, but the area that has seen the most recent population growth has been the south of Britain, due to transport links for trade with Europe and, more recently, due to migration from Europe and beyond.

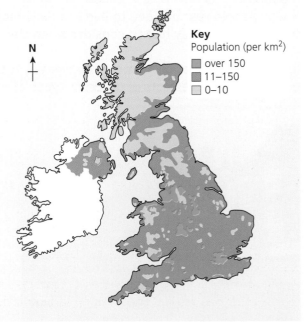

Key
Population (per km²)
- over 150
- 11–150
- 0–10

■ **Figure 2.4:** Population distribution in the United Kingdom

Living in different places

Look at Figures 2.5 and 2.6 and ask yourself:

- Would you like to live here?
- What would be the benefits of living in such a place?
- What would be some of the problems you might face living here?
- Which kind of people would most like to live here?

■ **Figure 2.5:** A busy street scene in central London

The census

Apart from looking at population distribution maps of the United Kingdom, how do we truly know how many people live where? The census is a large survey conducted by the government every ten years. It asks everybody in the United Kingdom questions about their lives and is a very important measure which is used in the future planning of essential services such as schools and hospitals at a local, regional and national level. The last census was in 2011. It revealed lots of interesting facts about the United Kingdom's population, including the mix of ethnic groups and religion. Look at the information in Figure 2.7 below. Notice that we have the third highest population in Europe but are, of course, much smaller in land size than both France and Germany.

■ **Figure 2.6:** A settlement in rural Scotland

Total population of the United Kingdom	Over 63 million
Total population compared to other EU countries	3rd highest behind Germany and France
London's average population density	5200 people per square kilometre
Ethnic groupings	87% White/7% Asian/3% Black/3% other
Religion	59% Christian/25% no religion/5% Muslim

■ **Figure 2.7:** 2011 census information for the United Kingdom

Population distribution across the globe

People are literally living on top of each other in London, with the 2011 census showing that the average population density in our capital city is 5200 people per square kilometre. This is nothing, however, compared to some other urban areas across the world. Some countries are experiencing rapid population growth. Have a look at Figure 2.8. In Dhaka, the capital city of Bangladesh, the population density is a staggering 45 000 people per square kilometre; that's nine times as many people as London squeezed into each square kilometre! Recently the total global population passed the 7 billion people mark.

Let's take a closer look at how the global population is spread across the globe and ask ourselves why in some places an incredible 45 000 people live in each square kilometre of land, while other areas of the globe remain uninhabited, as shown in Figure 2.9.

Two patterns emerge when you look at Figure 2.10 on page 31, which shows the distribution of the world's population. Firstly, all over the world populations have grown along the coastlines. This is because, alongside farming, fishing is a vital and traditional industry which provides food and livelihoods for many people in countries that have a coastline. Secondly, the highest population is centred in two different groups of countries:

■ **Figure 2.8:** A typical Dhaka street scene

■ **Figure 2.9:** The Siberian wilderness

● Developing nations in central and East Asia, such as China, India and Indonesia.
● Wealthier developed nations in Western Europe and North America.

One obvious reason why a country's total population rises is because more babies are being born (**birth rate**) than people dying (**death rate**). This is called **natural increase**. Natural increase is causing the populations of many developing countries to grow rapidly. In these countries families continue to have many children, often due to a lack of education and availability of contraception. At the same time death rates, although still high compared to more wealthy nations, are falling due to charities such as the Red Cross making vaccinations against deadly diseases available (see Figure 2.11). Unfortunately, in the world's poorest countries, natural increase is not as rapid, as basic medicines are still not being provided to people who need them. Therefore in countries such as Sierra Leone in Africa, the death rate remains relatively high.

A country's population may also increase due to people moving into the country. This may be the cause of population growth in some Western European countries such as Britain, where natural

■ **Figure 2.10:** Satellite map showing the world at night. The bright areas are densely populated.

increase is relatively low compared to developing countries such as Indonesia. Historically, early settlers built settlements in Western Europe and North America due to the favourable soil and climatic conditions for farming. After this the Industrial Revolution and trade between countries in these regions, combined with maturing colonies in Africa and Asia, meant populations in Western Europe and North America grew through the 19th century. More recently lifestyle choices have seen most families have fewer children. Therefore natural increase has slowed dramatically, despite a fall in the death rate due to advances in medicine.

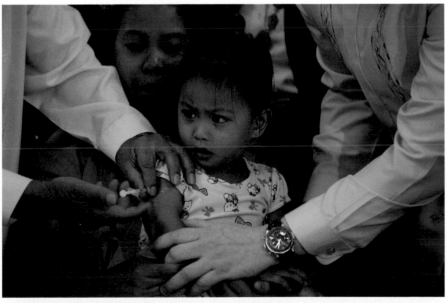

■ **Figure 2.11:** Child vaccination in the developing world

1   Is the area you live in sparsely populated or densely populated? Give at least two reasons why you think it is sparsely or densely populated.

2   Look at Figure 2.5 on page 29. Draw a mind map with a picture of you and your family at the middle. For each leg answer the following questions:

- Would you like to live here?
- What would be the benefits of living in such a place?
- What would be some of the problems you might face living here?
- Which kind of people would most like to live here?

3   Look at Figure 2.6 on page 29. Draw a mind map with a picture of you and your family at the middle. For each leg answer the following questions.

- Would you like to live here?
- What would be the benefits of living in such a place?
- What would be some of the problems you might face living here?
- Which kind of people would most like to live here?

Extension questions

4   Describe and explain two reasons why we generally find the population in the United Kingdom to be sparse in the north and west, and dense in the south and east.

5   (a)   What is the census and how often is it conducted?

    (b)   What did the 2011 census reveal about the United Kingdom's population?

6   Why is the world's population not evenly distributed?
    Use the following terms in your answer and refer to specific locations (you may wish to use an atlas to help you):

- birth rate
- death rate
- natural increase.

2.2 The population explosion and what it means for the future

What is the 'population explosion'?

Have a look at Figure 2.12 below. It shows how the world's population has grown over the last 12 000 years. It is fairly obvious that the world's total population has rapidly grown to its current figure of over 7 billion only very recently. This very fast growth is called the population explosion.

Dramatic growth began in around 1950, as global food production grew with wide use of pesticides and machinery, but it has continued to shoot up at an accelerating rate to the present day. Population growth varies significantly from one region of the world to another and is most prominent in the developing world. For example, Indonesia's population grew from 97 million in 1961 to 237.6 million in 2011, an increase of 145 per cent in 49 years. In India, the population grew from 361.1 million people in 1951, to just over 1.2 billion by 2011, an increase of 235 per cent in 60 years.

As for the future, many projection models have been used to predict whether global population levels will continue to rise as they have done in the last three centuries. Most projections show that the world population will continue to grow until at least 2050, with the population reaching 9 billion in 2040 and some predictions putting the population in 2050 as high as 11 billion. According to the United Nations' World Population Prospects report:

- The world population is currently growing by approximately 74 million people per year.
- Almost all growth will take place in the less developed regions, where today's 5.3 billion population in underdeveloped countries is expected to increase to 7.8 billion in 2050.
- The population of the more developed regions will remain mostly unchanged, at 1.2 billion.

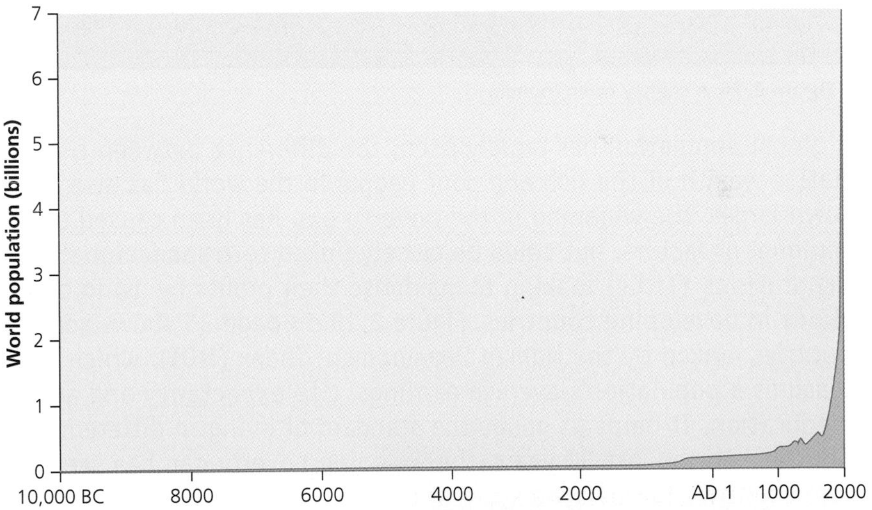

■ **Figure 2.12:** Global population growth

Why should we be concerned about the population explosion?

World leaders, scientists and charity groups are all concerned about the results of the population explosion, in particular overpopulation. Overpopulation is when a region has so many people it cannot support them with their basic needs, such as food, fresh clean water and shelter. This can cause terrible human suffering in the form of famine and malnutrition, as shown in Figure 2.13. Inadequate

■ **Figure 2.13:** A baby with malnutrition

space and government money to provide housing for growing populations in developing countries can lead to shanty towns forming in urban areas, such as that shown in Figure 2.14. These self-built, densely populated settlements are dirty and dangerous due to a lack of basic sanitation services and no planning laws.

■ **Figure 2.14:** A shanty town in India

As global population has rapidly risen, the difference between the relative wealth of the rich and poor people in the world has also grown larger. The widening of the poverty gap has been caused by a number of factors, but could be closely linked to transnational corporations (TNCs) looking to maximise their profits by using cheap labour in developing countries. Figure 2.15 on page 35 shows some countries ranked by the Human Development Index (HDI), which measures a population's average earnings, life expectancy and access to education. It helps us gauge the standard of living in different countries. In the last 30 years, the widening poverty gap has seen more countries fall below a score of 0.4 on the HDI. At the same time, a greater number of wealthy countries have risen to a score above 0.9. Governments in developed countries are also concerned about overpopulation in developing countries, as they contribute heavily towards the aid given to them to help the world's poorest people. Food supplies and medicines are provided through funds provided by Western governments, as well as independently through humanitarian charities such as the Red Cross.

HDI rank	HDI	Country	Life expectancy	Expected years of schooling	GNI ($)
1	0.955	Norway	81.3	17.5	48688
2	0.938	Australia	82	19.6	34340
3	0.937	United States	78.7	16.8	43480
4	0.921	Netherlands	80.8	16.9	37282
5	0.92	Germany	80.6	16.4	35431
27	0.875	United Kingdom	80.3	16.4	32538
182	0.343	Burkina Faso	55.9	6.9	1202
183	0.34	Chad	49.9	7.4	1258
184	0.327	Mozambique	50.7	9.2	906
185	0.304	Congo	48.7	8.5	319
186	0.304	Niger	55.1	4.9	701

■ **Figure 2.15:** Table of countries by HDI rating

As the global population continues to rise, so does the demand for energy. Although wealthier Western nations, such as the United Kingdom, are investing in green energy, such as wind farms and hydroelectric power (HEP), countries which are experiencing their industrial revolutions now (NICs) tend to gain their energy from fossil fuels, as shown in Figure 2.16. Towards the end of the 20th century and start of the 21st century, many more countries in the developing world are becoming NICs whose industries and populations are demanding more and more energy. Add to this the demand for energy being amplified in developed countries, where the technological revolution has created a surge in demand for electricity, and we are now experiencing an unprecedented global demand for energy at a time when we are really beginning to feel the impact of climate change.

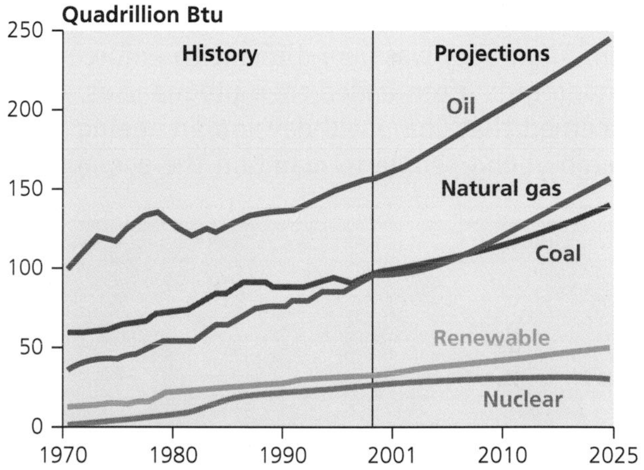

■ **Figure 2.16:** Global rise in different types of energy

Can global population growth be controlled?

You may have noticed that there is no such thing as a 'global government'. So how can we possibly control a global problem like overpopulation? Such major issues are discussed by world leaders when they meet at the United Nations (see Figure 2.17) where ideas and possible solutions are debated and, occasionally, agreements made.

Some governments have taken direct action to reduce the population growth in their country, and therefore reduce the drain on basic resources such as food and energy. China, for example, limited its population to having only one child per couple following a rapid increase in its birth rate in the middle of the 20th century. Figure 2.18 shows some of the advantages and disadvantages of this approach to population control, which is an extreme solution which many people feel infringes upon the human rights of China's people. A more common solution adopted across the developing world, where birth rates continue to soar, is education regarding methods of birth control. The main barrier to this remains religious or tribal beliefs that birth control should not be practised.

■ **Figure 2.17:** The United Nations headquarters in New York

China's birth rate fell by 30 per cent in 20 years. The overall population is estimated to be 230 million less than it would have been. The policy was very difficult to enforce in rural areas. Women carrying girls often ended their pregnancies. Officials are now concerned that China will develop an ageing population without enough young people to maintain the economy.

■ **Figure 2.18:** Benefits and problems of China's one child policy

Exercise 2B

1 (a) Write a sentence to explain what the population explosion is.

   (b) Draw two large arrows pointing upwards. In the point of the first arrow write the current world population figure. In the point of the second arrow write the projected global population in 2050.

(c) Now add some speech bubbles to the arrows which describe what effect rising global population levels will have on the planet and its population.

2 List the names of three countries which have HDI scores above 0.9 and three countries which have HDI scores below 0.4.

3 Why should we be concerned about increased demand for energy as the world population grows? Use the following terms in your answer:

- fossil fuels
- green energy
- Newly Industrialised Countries (NICs).

Extension questions

4 Explain the meaning of the 'poverty gap' and discuss what you think can be done to reduce the gap between the rich and the poor.

5 Was China's 'one child per couple' policy successful? Write at least three sentences to describe its impact.

6 If you were a leader of a developing country with a high birth rate, what would you do to try and manage future problems?

2.3 The site and situation of a settlement

A background to settlements in Britain

There was a time when Britain was populated by tribes that may have occupied a region but did not live permanently in one place. Instead, these tribes moved around the region hunting and gathering food. A mobile population such as this is known as **nomadic**, and such communities still exist in many parts of the world.

However, approximately 10 000 years ago these nomadic populations developed the ability to grow crops from seed, rather than just gather edible wild vegetation, and rear animals for their young. Thus farming, or **agriculture** as we know it today, began. Growing crops from seed and rearing animals in enclosures required these previously nomadic populations to stay in one place, and therefore the first settlements were developed.

Soon after people settled in one place they began to trade. Most farmers grew crops and reared animals for consumption by their own family. This method of farming is called **subsistence farming**. However, during a good season a farmer may produce too many crops; this extra produce is called a **surplus**. Rather than let it go to waste a farmer would rather sell his surplus within his settlement, or more likely, to people from other settlements who had not produced as much. This, in turn, led to trade between settlements and the development of early transport routes between settlements, many of which form the basis of roads we use today.

When we begin to think about the reasons why a certain place was chosen for a settlement it is important to remember that many settlements are very old. This is especially true in Britain, as many of our settlements were first built hundreds if not thousands of years ago. For example, the two OS map extracts in this chapter (pages 62 and 63) are of Sheffield which is believed to have been founded in the 12th century, although there are many older examples than this in Britain.

Site factors

When early settlers were choosing a suitable place to build a settlement, they would have considered various factors. These site factors (see Figure 2.19), were likely to be related to the physical landscape of the area.

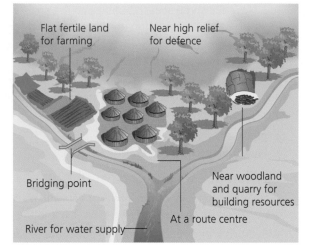

■ **Figure 2.19:** A sketch illustrating the six site factors

Water supply

Unlike today, piped water was not readily available from a tap and a fresh water supply was vital for a settlement to exist. Rivers were generally less polluted than they are today and were an obvious supply of fresh water, as were springs and wells.

Defence

Settling populations needed to consider defending themselves against other rival tribes in the region and later against invading armies from Europe. A site on the inside of a river meander or near or on a hill-top is easier to defend than other locations.

Bridging points/fords

Settlers were likely to cross a river at a shallow point and then build a bridge in this position. Once established, a bridge would act as a trading route for settlements situated either side of the river.

Route centres and transport

Certain locations have been natural route meeting points for thousands of years due to their physical landscape. For example, the routes used by locals and traders at the bottom of valleys meet where two or more valleys converge. These ancient routes may have developed into modern roads and the route centres into large settlements.

Farming

A site that offered flat land either side of a river (floodplain) would be attractive to early settlers as farming was a necessity to feed people. Being too close to the river would bring the danger of flooding, however, so settlements were often located higher up the floodplain. Due to the growth of settlements most modern settlements have now built on their floodplains.

Building materials and fuel

Early societies needed easily accessible resources close by. Proximity to woodland was useful as timber could be used for several purposes including house building, boat construction and as a fuel for cooking and heating. Easily quarried stone was also a valuable resource for building.

Situation

The site of a settlement is its exact location (originally resulting from various advantages of that location). However, the physical geography of the land surrounding the settlement was also important to early settlers and this is called the situation of a settlement. If a settlement had several good site factors and a good situation, such as Sheffield (see OS map on pages 62 and 63 and Figure 2.20) it had the potential to grow into a large city. A settlement with similarly good site factors may be prevented from growing by a limited situation. For example, Oughtibridge (see OS map on page 63 and Figure 2.21 on page 40) has several good site factors such as a bridging point, a route centre and a river but its situation has limited its growth as it is surrounded by steep-sided valley slopes.

You may like to consider the site and the situation of your school.

The site and situation of Sheffield

Sheffield has grown into a large city with a population recorded at the 2001 census of 513 234. Like all settlements, it started with just a few houses and a very small population, but Sheffield has grown due to some of the following site and situation factors. Use the OS map on page 62 to identify each one.

1. It has a water supply in the River Don (grid square (GS): 3291).

2. It has high ground which would have been useful for defence (GS: 3489).

3. It has a series of bridging points (GS: 3588).

4. It is a natural route centre located at the head of three valleys – the River Don, River Loxley and River Riveline (GS: 3289/3489).

5. The floodplain of the River Don would have provided excellent farmland, although it has now been developed (GS: 3888).

6. There are woodlands surrounding Sheffield (GS: 3294).

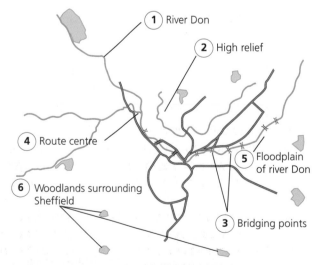

■ **Figure 2.20:** An annotated sketch map showing Sheffield's site factors and situation

It is not always possible fully to identify reasons for a settlement's growth from a map. Sheffield grew initially due to the wool trade in the 13th century, using wool from sheep grazing on the Pennines. Later, with the advent of the Industrial Revolution in the late 18th and early 19th century, Sheffield's population increased rapidly when people from surrounding rural areas came to live in Sheffield and work in the iron and steel factories.

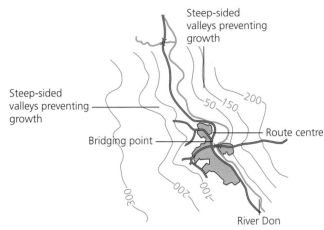

■ **Figure 2.21:** An annotated sketch map showing Oughtibridge's site factors and situation

→ **Exam tip**

When answering an exam question about the original site factors of a settlement, think about what would have happened in the past. You are likely to be asked to quote evidence from an OS map to support your answer; look for castles, rivers, cathedrals, bridging points and route centres.

Exercise 2C

1 Explain why people decided to live in a fixed place in Britain 10 000 years ago.

2 What does the term 'surplus' mean?

3 For what reasons do you think Sheffield grew into the city of over half a million people that it is today?

4 Why has Oughtibridge not grown in the same way that Sheffield has?

5 Look at the OS maps in this book of settlements other than Sheffield (pages 23–26). Try to identify the original site factors for another settlement.

Extension questions

6 Why did agriculture replace a nomadic life for those living in Britain 10 000 years ago?

7 Explain how agricultural surpluses led to trade between settlements.

8 Explain why some settlements grow steadily over the centuries whereas others show very little population change. Refer to examples in your answer.

9 Settlements may appear to be randomly scattered on our landscape. Is this the case?

2.4 Settlement patterns and functions

Settlement patterns

There are three principal <u>settlement patterns</u> or shapes (see Figure 2.22 on page 42):

- **<u>linear settlements</u>**, where the buildings are arranged in a line
- **<u>nucleated settlements</u>**, where the buildings are arranged around a central point
- **<u>dispersed settlements</u>**, where the buildings are few in number and well away from other settlements.

It is very difficult to know what pattern a settlement is when you are actually in, or driving through, that settlement. However, if you see the settlement from above, the bird's eye or **plan view**, it becomes a lot clearer. You might have seen settlement patterns from above when looking out of the window of an aeroplane, but the easiest way to see the pattern of a settlement is by looking at a map.

Many settlements in Britain fit into these three categories of settlement pattern and there are few new settlements being built; it is much more likely that older settlements will expand. However, there is another category called **planned settlements**, where new settlements are built from scratch and in a well planned, ordered fashion. Such new planned settlements are found in developed and developing countries and often include grid pattern roads and many roundabouts (for example Milton Keynes in Britain).

Reasons for settlement patterns

Just as there is always a reason why a settlement is first settled, there is always a good reason why it grows in the pattern it does.

Nucleated comes from the word 'nucleus' meaning a core or central point. Nucleated settlements can grow around a number of different features at their core. Very commonly this may be a crossroads where people have decided to settle and trade. Smaller nucleated villages may have a village green at their core, which would have served as a <u>market</u> place in years gone by but is most likely to be used for recreation today. Nucleated settlements could also be built around such features as a river confluence, a bridging point or ford, a castle, a cathedral or a market place.

Linear comes from the word 'line'. A linear settlement, or **ribbon settlement**, is arranged in a line, though this does not have to be a straight line. The most common place to find linear settlements is along a main road leading to a large settlement or on a main road between two larger settlements. Linear settlements may also be found tracing the course of a river along the bottom of a valley. The presence of the sea means that along coastlines, settlements sometimes spread out in a linear fashion. Along the shores of large lakes, settlements grow in a

Nucleated

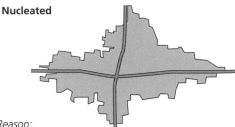

Reason:
- Crossroads • Market place • Castle at centre
- Bridging point/ford • Village green
- River confluence • Cathedral at centre

■ **Figure 2.22** (i): A nucleated settlement – Bisley, Gloucestershire

Linear

Reason:
- Road between two larger settlements • River
- Valley bottom • Coast/large lake frontage

■ **Figure 2.22** (ii): A linear settlement – Brooksby, Leicestershire

Dispersed

Reason:
- Farmland • High relief
- Physical landscape (forest/lakes/desert)

■ **Figure 2.22** (iii): A dispersed settlement – Little Haresfield, Gloucestershire

linear fashion to make the most of waterside frontage (for example, Lake Leman, Switzerland).

Dispersed means 'spread out'. Dispersed settlements are located in rural areas away from other settlements. They may be made up of just a few houses or may be of hamlet size, but there is always a reason for their distance from other settlements. In Britain this is usually because the land is needed for farming so cannot be built on. However, it is often the physical landscape that limits the growth of settlements and this causes the settlement pattern to be dispersed. Dense forest causes settlements to be dispersed

■ **Figure 2.23:** A centre for commerce and leisure

in tropical areas such as Brazil, high relief is the cause in mountainous countries such as Nepal, a high density of lakes is the cause in countries like Finland, and a barren desert landscape causes settlements to be dispersed in regions such as the Sahara in western Africa.

Settlement functions

The functions of a settlement are the purpose of a settlement and often explain why it has grown: the things that happen there. The functions of settlements may be split into six groups. A settlement may begin with just one function and then over time develop more functions. The functions of a settlement may change as well as grow.

Commercial

Most settlements have some form of commercial function. This means they have shopping facilities ranging from a small shop in a village to shopping malls in towns and cities. Commercial functions can also include facilities such as cinemas and sports centres.

Residential

All settlements have a residential function. However, some settlements are built purposely to provide homes for people, often outside a city due to overcrowding in the centre. Dormitory settlements are settlements that are close to larger settlements and where many of the inhabitants commute into the city to work each day.

Administrative

Larger settlements often have an administrative function. This means that local government has central offices in the settlement from which it runs public services such as waste disposal and library services.

Industrial

Settlements of all different sizes may have an industrial function. This means that companies that make (manufacture) something locate their factory in the settlement. Big cities tend to have many industries because these industries need a lot of people to work in their factories. However, some industries may wish to locate near smaller settlements because the land price may be cheaper.

Tourism

Different kinds of settlement may have a tourist function due to different reasons. Big cities have the attraction of museums, art galleries and major sports facilities. Small villages in beautiful countryside have the attraction of outside sports and the quiet rural life.

Services

As the size of a settlement increases, the range and number of services increase. Services include things such as doctors' surgeries, hospitals and schools. A small village may have none of these services, whereas a major city will have many.

> **Exam tip**
>
> When identifying the pattern of a settlement on an OS map, try to identify the cause of the settlement growing in this pattern because if you can find the cause you are probably right about which pattern it is.
>
> If you are asked to identify the functions of a settlement from an OS map, even if it is in an extremely rural area, the settlement will have a residential function as all settlements have this function.

Exercise 2D

1 Draw simple diagrams to show the three settlement patterns.

2 For each settlement pattern describe what could cause the settlement to have grown like this.

3 What is meant by the term 'settlement function'?

4 What are the functions of your local town or city? What evidence do you have to support your answer?

5 Use the OS map extract of Sheffield (pages 62 and 63) to find evidence of Sheffield's functions. Give a four figure grid reference for each piece of evidence.

6 Name two places in the world that have mostly dispersed settlements. Explain your choices.

Extension questions

7 Look at the OS map extract of Sheffield (pages 62 and 63). Find a linear settlement and draw a sketch of it including details such as buildings, roads, rivers and contour lines. Give your sketch a clear title.

8 Give the six figure grid reference of any dispersed settlements on the map. Identify why you think they are dispersed. Quote map evidence in your answer.

9 Why are nucleated settlements the most common type of settlement? Illustrate your answer with examples.

◯ 2.5 The settlement hierarchy, shops and services

Settlements in a hierarchy

The word <u>hierarchy</u> describes putting things in order, giving something a rank or priority. It can be applied to different subjects. For example, you rank football teams by which division they are in and, within their divisions, by how many points they have. The football hierarchy is seen as tables but hierarchies are more commonly represented as pyramids (see Figure 2.24). Using a pyramid with bands to split it, it should be possible for you to create a hierarchy of people within your school with the headteacher at the top.

Broadly, we split the settlement hierarchy up into four, with cities in the top band of the hierarchy, followed by towns, villages and then hamlets. As the pyramid indicates, the further you go up the settlement hierarchy the more important the settlement will be, as it will have more services and functions. As you go down the hierarchy the frequency or number of settlements increases. So there will be more hamlets than villages, more villages than towns and so on.

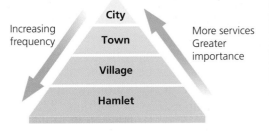

■ **Figure 2.24:** The settlement hierarchy

City, town, village or hamlet?

Deciding whether a settlement is a city, town, village or hamlet is not as simple as you may think, and those in power within local and central government both influence this process of categorising settlements. Three factors are taken into consideration:

- the population size of the settlement
- the number of services the settlement offers and how far people will come to use these services (the **range**).
- the distance the settlement is from other settlements. Therefore, large settlements such as cities will be far apart from each other, whereas smaller settlements such as hamlets could be very close to other hamlets.

These three factors are summarised below:

	Cities	Towns	Villages	Hamlets
Typical services	MANY			FEW
	Many schools Shopping complex University Cathedral Hospitals Sports stadiums Many hotels Department stores	Railway station Town hall Cinema Shopping arcade Secondary schools Bus station Banks	Doctor's surgery Primary school Public house Village hall	None
Typical population	HIGH			LOW
	Over 100 000	1000 to 100 000	20 to 1000	Under 20
Typical distance apart	FAR			NEAR
	Up to 160 km (100 miles)	40–80 km (25–50 miles)	8–16 km (5–10 miles)	1.5–3 km (1–2 miles)

■ **Figure 2.25:** Categorising settlements

Look at the OS map extracts of Sheffield on pages 60 and 61. The settlement hierarchy is evident on this map. There is one city (Sheffield) which is surrounded by several villages (Thorpe Hesley 3796, Dungworth 2889, etc.) and many hamlets (Storrs 2989, Hollow Meadows 2488, etc.) in the rural area beyond the city limits. Chapeltown 3596 is not a town but is in fact a <u>suburb</u> of the city of Sheffield. There are no towns on the OS map extract of Sheffield. Why do you think this is?

Shops and services

Have you ever thought about what type of shops and services you get in different types of settlement? You may have noticed that in villages you often only find a newsagent and a primary school whereas large towns or cities have big department stores, restaurants, hotels, cinemas and many more different shops and services.

A summary of the shops and services offered by a typical settlement at each band of the settlement hierarchy is shown in Figure 2.25 on page 45.

A minimum population level is necessary for a settlement to support different shops and services. This minimum population number is called the **threshold**. For example, to have a village shop it is estimated that a village must have at least 300 people living in it (a threshold of 300 people). The threshold for a large department store such as Debenhams is much higher, demanding a minimum population of nearer 100 000 people. Therefore we only see department stores in cities.

A local convenience shop

A large department store

■ **Figure 2.26:** Outlets for convenience goods and comparison goods

The range of a shop is the distance people are prepared to travel to reach it and the **catchment area** is where those people are living. The range depends on the type of goods the shop is selling. A village shop sells goods that we buy on a daily basis such as bread, milk and newspapers. We call these **convenience goods** and would not be prepared to travel very far to buy them. A village shop selling convenience goods would therefore have a small range and would be called a low order service. An electrical shop sells much more expensive items such as personal computers and DVD players. Customers will compare the price of these items at other electrical shops before buying. We call these **comparison goods**, and customers would travel into the city to buy them. A shop selling comparison goods, said to be a high order service, would therefore have a large range.

Public services such as libraries, schools and hospitals also have a threshold and range. You might expect to find a primary school in a village as it will have a low threshold and small range. However, you would expect to find a large hospital in a city because it has a high threshold and large range. For example, Sheffield has a large hospital. Look at the OS map extract on page 60, grid square 3690.

Managing urban development: Meadowhall, Sheffield

We all know that if you want to go shopping in most settlements you head for the town or city centre, which we call the Central Business District (CBD). But not all shops are found in the middle of the city; in fact since 1980 there has been a steady increase in the number of out of town shopping centres being built in or beyond the **outer suburbs** of Britain's cities.

Out of town shopping centres are large developments of shops, restaurants and entertainment facilities that are built on sites away from the city because of the specific advantages of these locations, some of which are listed below.

- Close to a motorway junction providing good access to a large catchment area.
- Close to an **arterial road** linking the out of town shopping centre with the CBD and other areas of the nearest city, or a bypass making it accessible to the surrounding area.
- Built on cheaper land as it is away from the centre of the city.
- Built on a site with lots of space available for parking.

Out of town shopping centres have a large range and attract customers from urban areas across a large region. However, they are normally located in, or just beyond, the outer suburbs of one particular city, and therefore might take business away from shops located in the CBD of that city. There may be some positive effects of fewer people visiting the CBD such as less traffic congestion and less pollution, but negative effects include unemployment in the CBD and vandalism of shops that have been boarded up after closing down.

On the OS map extract of Sheffield on page 60 you can see Meadowhall shopping centre at grid reference 393900. Meadowhall was built on this site in 1990 and boasts over 270 different shops, its own cinema and a food court. It has excellent transport links with the rest of Sheffield, having its own train and tram stations, as well as being located on one of the main bus and car routes into the centre of Sheffield. The nearby motorway junction of the M1 means that Meadowhall is within one hour's drive of nine other cities including Rotherham, Doncaster and Barnsley.

Figure 2.30 below shows an aerial view of Meadowhall. Planners took careful consideration of the environment when planning and building the centre. The site was approved for development as it was a **brownfield site** which had previously been a steelworks and lay derelict. To avoid **visual pollution** and to maximise the available land, Meadowhall was constructed only two storeys high. As the text accompanying Figure 2.27 shows, Meadowhall's management has further considered the environment by operating a major **recycling** scheme, which sees 95 per cent of waste recycled, and by using rainwater for flushing the toilets.

You can find out more about Meadowhall by looking at its website: www.meadowhall.co.uk

---

Doing our bit

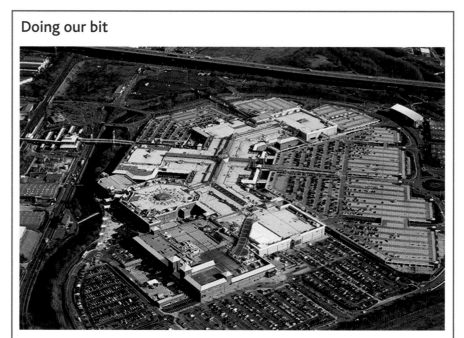

■ **Figure 2.27:** Meadowhall

We believe in doing our bit towards making the world a better kind of place for us all. That's why we have policies on everything from giving the people who work at Meadowhall the training they want to recycling as much as we possibly can. We call it 'Doing the right thing' and this means doing it for everyone – from our retailers to our shoppers and from the people of Sheffield to the citizens of the world!

- We're the first shopping centre to have our very own recycling centre which swallows up a massive 95% of our waste and saves it from heading for landfill sites.

- We collect rainwater to flush hundreds of toilets and water thousands of plants all round the centre.
- We make it easy for people to leave the car at home and visit us by foot, bike, bus, train or tram.
- We were the first shopping centre in the UK and the first location in Sheffield to install electric car charging points. Our recharging points are easily identified by the green bays located in the management car park; this facility can be used free of charge. The Meadowhall EV recharging point project was made possible through partnership with Sheffield City Council and grant funding contributions from the Energy Savings Trust.

These are just a few ways we're being greener – and we could tell you lots more besides.

www.meadowhall.co.uk

Since Meadowhall opened in 1990 it has been reported that takings at shops in Sheffield's CBD have been reduced by 25 per cent and many have been forced to close down. Empty shops have been targeted by graffiti and therefore make the city centre less attractive, which in turn deters new businesses from starting up in the CBD.

Smaller settlements have shops selling convenience goods because they have a low threshold and small range. Larger settlements will have shops selling comparison goods because they have a high threshold and large range. These settlements may have out of town shopping centres in their suburbs which may take business away from shops in the CBD.

Exercise 2E

1 Make a simple copy of Figure 2.24 (page 45). Add to it an example of a hamlet, village, town and city from your local area.

2 Look at the OS map extract of Sheffield on page 60. In grid square 3092 you will see a settlement called Worrall. What type of settlement is this: a hamlet, village, town or city? Give reasons for your answer referring to map evidence.

3 OS maps do not show individual shops so we cannot tell what shops there are in Worrall. Would you expect to find convenience or comparison goods for sale in a shop in Worrall? Give a reason for your answer using the terms 'threshold' and 'range'.

4 Draw a spider diagram to show the advantages of the site that was chosen for the location of Meadowhall shopping centre (see the OS map extract of Sheffield on page 60, grid reference 393909).

5 What problems can the building of out of town shopping centres in the city suburbs have on the CBD of the city?

Extension questions

6 Rearrange the settlements in the South Yorkshire extract (see Figure 2.28) into a triangular settlement hierarchy as in Figure 2.24 (page 45).

7 Look at the OS map extract of Sheffield on pages 60 and 61. If Debenhams were going to build a new department store in this area, in which of the following grid squares do you think it would be put: 3092, 3990 or 3587? Discuss the advantages and disadvantages of each site using some of the following terms: hierarchy; range or catchment area; threshold; convenience goods or low order services; comparison goods or high order services; Central Business District.

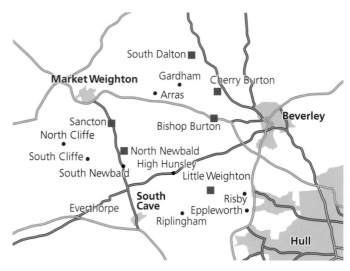

■ **Figure 2.28:** Settlements in South Yorkshire

8 Use the OS map extract of Sheffield on page 60 to identify specific map evidence that shows why Meadowhall shopping centre was built where it was. Can you identify any other sites on the OS map extract of Sheffield (pages 60 and 61) that might have been suitable for an out of town shopping centre? Give reasons for your choices.

9 Draw a flow chart to illustrate the problems that can be caused for businesses and the environment in the CBD when an out of town shopping centre opens in the suburbs of the city.

2.6 Urban land use patterns in Britain

Land use in urban areas

Land use is the way the land is utilised, whether it is for housing, offices, factories, entertainment facilities, colleges or universities, or simply left as open parkland. Urban areas, our towns and cities, have many different land uses which can change very quickly as you move from one part of a town or city to another. Think about your nearest urban area. Can you identify how the land use changes from one part of this town or city to another? Although all cities are different you may be surprised to learn that they often have very similar land uses which are often located in very similar parts of the city. Because of this, geographers have been able to create a general diagram, called a model, which shows what the different land uses in different parts of an average city might be. In this model, a simple and clear pattern emerges, showing changing land use in a circular pattern coming out from the city centre (the CBD).

The concentric circle model

You have already seen a geographical model in the form of a settlement hierarchy (see page 45). Models are simplified versions of reality, therefore no region will fit perfectly into the settlement hierarchy and no city will fit perfectly into the pattern the concentric circle model suggests (see Figure 2.29). This model applies to cities in developed countries; a different model needs to be drawn for the land use pattern in developing countries. Here we see four parts of the city and how three patterns emerge as you travel from the outskirts of the city towards the CBD.

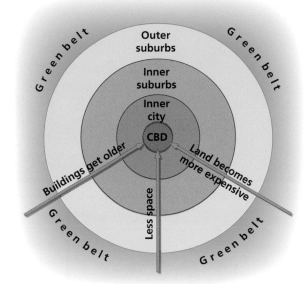

■ **Figure 2.29:** The concentric circle model

- Without redevelopment the age of buildings increases. The oldest buildings will be in the centre where the city began.
- Land becomes more expensive as more value is placed on property within easy reach of the facilities of the CBD. Land in the CBD is too valuable for housing.
- The amount of space decreases as housing becomes more compact nearer to the CBD, in order to allow as many people as possible to have a short commute to the CBD.

Land use in the concentric circle model

The simplest concentric circle model has four parts. Figure 2.30 shows what the land use might be in each of the four parts of the city. The very centre of the city is known as the CBD. This is likely to be where the city first started and you may be able to find map evidence for this, such as a bridging point or

CBD	Inner city	Inner suburbs	Outer suburbs	Country-side
• Old buildings	• Terraced housing	• Semi-detached housing	• Detached houses	• Farmland
• Modernised buildings	• Flats	• Convenience goods shops	• Hospitals	• Green belt
• Shops	• Converted factories	• Schools	• Out of town shopping centres	
• Offices	• Modernised housing		• Park land	
• Entertainment	• Art galleries		• Stadiums	
• Restaurants			• Industrial estates	
• Train/bus station			• Ring road	
• Flats				

■ **Figure 2.30:** Land use in each part of the concentric circle model

CBD – civic amenities

Inner city – terraced housing

Inner suburbs – semi-detached housing

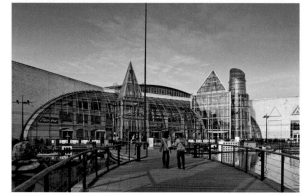
Outer suburbs – a shopping centre

■ **Figure 2.31:** Land use from each part of the concentric circle model

route centre. The CBD may contain old buildings as it was the likely starting point of the city but will also have modern buildings and old buildings that have been **modernised**. The CBD will have lots of shops, restaurants and entertainment facilities such as nightclubs and bars. It will also have office blocks but very little if any land in the CBD will be given to housing, which might be in apartment blocks due to the very limited space available. The CBD will be the meeting point for transport routes in the city so you will find train, bus and tram stations all located in, or close to, the CBD.

Moving away from the CBD, the next zone in the concentric circle model is called the **inner city**. Typically you will find <u>terraced housing</u> in this zone. These houses are small, arranged in rows and old as they were built to accommodate factory workers during the Industrial Revolution. Factories have since relocated to the outer suburbs due to the cheaper land and space for expansion. Old factories, commonly mills, have therefore been converted into other land uses such as housing, museums or art galleries, a process known as **urban renewal**. The Tate Modern art gallery, located in London's inner city zone, was a former power station which closed in 1982.

The **inner suburbs** form the next zone of the city. The land in the inner suburbs is mostly given to housing. As there is more space in the inner suburbs the housing tends to be larger and **semi-detached**, and many of the houses have gardens and garages. As this zone of the city has been built more recently, housing also tends to be newer and is occasionally accompanied by schools and shops selling convenience goods.

The final outer zone of the city is called the outer suburbs. There are a variety of different land uses in this zone because there is a lot more space, the land is cheaper and ring roads give good access. Houses in the outer suburbs tend to be large and <u>detached</u> and have large gardens. The outer suburbs may also contain sports stadiums, hospitals, universities, council estates, industrial estates and out of town shopping centres.

Limiting urban growth

Strict laws are in place in most developing countries to prevent cities growing out of control. If there were no such laws, cities would continually spread outwards, a process known as urban sprawl or <u>urbanisation</u>. When planning laws were less strict in Britain, urban sprawl led to cities that were once many miles apart growing together to form one large urban area called a **conurbation**. For example, in Britain, Manchester and Liverpool have grown together, as have Leeds and Bradford. There are many planning laws set down by central and local government but the most well-known is the **green belt**. The green belt is an area surrounding a city within which you have to have very special permission to build new property, or even to change the shape or use of existing property.

Does Sheffield fit the concentric circle model?

Not all cities fit the patterns shown by the concentric circle model. Often physical features such as the coastline or steep hills direct the growth of a city into a different shape. For example, cities close to the sea will spread along the coastline in a linear fashion. Mountains might hamper the growth of an urban area in a certain direction. Folkestone in Kent is limited by steep relief in one direction and coastline in another.

Look at the OS map extract on pages 60 and 61. Do you think Sheffield fits the patterns shown in the concentric circle model? Certainly urban growth is limited to the west by high relief and the planning restrictions imposed by the national park (indicated by the yellow boundary). However, if you follow the A6135 from Sheffield's CBD to the outer suburbs you should find evidence that land use changes in a way that fits the concentric circle model.

1 Write at least two lines each to explain the meaning of the following terms, giving examples:

   (a) land use

   (b) geographical model

2 Make a larger copy of Figure 2.29 (page 51), adding some of the detail of land use in each zone from Figure 2.30 (page 51).

3 What patterns does the concentric circle model show about a typical city in a developed country?

4 How does the type of housing change as you travel from the outer suburbs towards the CBD?

5 What is urban sprawl and what can be done to prevent it? Use examples in your answer.

Extension questions

6 Write half a page to discuss the changes in land use that emerge as you travel from the outer suburbs towards the CBD. Indicate patterns that are evident and give examples of land use.

7 Why do you think we get shopping facilities in the CBD, but also often in the outer suburbs in out of town shopping centres?

8 Giving map evidence from the extracts on pages 60 and 61, explain whether you think Sheffield does or does not fit into the patterns shown by the concentric circle model.

9 Do you think your local town or city fits the concentric circle model? Give reasons for your answer.

10 Conurbations are a result of urban sprawl. Discuss this statement and refer to examples of planning law.

2.7 The effects of migration on settlements

What is migration?

Migration is the term used to describe the movement of people from one place to another. There are several types of migration. We call the groups of people involved in these different types of migration different names. It is important not to confuse them.

International migration is when people move from one country to another. This may be a permanent move for the rest of their lives or simply a temporary move for a number of months or years. All people moving from one place to another are called migrants. The process of moving from one country to another is called **emigration** and people who have moved into a country from their own are called **immigrants**.

Normally temporary migrants move to a different country because they are taking a job contract in that country. Such migrants have the choice to move so they are also referred to as voluntary migrants. You may have lived abroad with your parents because they decided to take a job in a different country for a period of time. Permanent migration is more likely to be the result of people seeking a better lifestyle or standard of living. Figure 2.32 gives more reasons for temporary and permanent migration.

What causes migration?

The causes of any form of migration can be split into <u>push factors</u>, reasons why people want to leave a place, and <u>pull factors</u>, reasons why people are attracted to a different place. These are listed in Figure 2.32. It is usually a combination of push and pull factors that causes voluntary migrants to migrate whether temporarily or permanently. A poor standard of living and lack of jobs are the most common push factors while the prospect of better paid jobs and a higher standard of services such as education and health are the most common pull factors. Sometimes a member of a family may have already emigrated to a different country and other family members follow.

Push factors	Pull factors
● War	● Better jobs
● Famine	● Attractive environment
● Natural disasters	● Better standard of living
● Unemployment	● Family members to join
● Drought	● Better education / health services

■ **Figure 2.32:** Push and pull factors

Unfortunately many migrants are forced to move either within a country or from one country to another due to problems where they live that are out of their control. These problems may include war, or natural disasters such as famine, **drought** or floods. These forced migrants are referred to as **refugees** (see Figure 2.33). People who enter another country for work or in search of a higher standard of living without permission are called **illegal immigrants**.

■ **Figure 2.33:** Refugees in Sudan as a result of famine

Migration in developing countries

Often natural disasters such as famine and man-made problems such as war occur in developing countries. Such events lead to **forced migration** with people leaving a region or country. Sometimes this may mean people are refugees in another country for a number of weeks or months but it may lead to permanent migration.

The most common process of migration in a developing country, however, is the movement of people from the countryside to the city; this is called **rural-urban migration**. It is a constant process and occurs because those living in rural areas, who are very poor and struggling to make a living from farming, believe they will be able to find a job and have a better standard of living in the city. Unfortunately, often migrants find there are few jobs available in the city for which they are qualified, and they are forced to make their own shelters to live in along with other migrants in what are called shanty towns (see Figure 2.34).

Migration in Britain

In Britain, a large amount of rural-urban migration took place in the 19th century during the Industrial Revolution. People left their homes and work as farmers in the countryside in their thousands and took jobs in factories located in towns and cities. From this time until very recently Britain's urban areas, its towns and cities, have continued to grow as people seek **employment** that they cannot find in rural areas.

However, in the last thirty years a new pattern has emerged. Many people are now deciding to leave the city and live in the countryside in order to enjoy a better environment. This process is called **counterurbanisation**. Many cities have become congested, polluted and blighted by crime and have become expensive and stressful places to live. Many people in Britain, particularly those who have children, have therefore decided to move to villages in rural areas. This has been made increasingly easier in the last thirty years for a number of reasons (see Figure 2.35).

Counterurbanisation has meant that many rural villages have seen significant new house building in recent years and subsequent swelling of their populations. Many villages, with their new housing estates, now look like the suburbs of a city and are therefore called **suburbanised villages**. With higher populations, such villages might have been expected to support more services such as shops, banks and primary schools, but in fact the opposite has occurred. Some services in suburbanised villages have actually decreased because most people in the village are commuters who use the services of the towns and cities they work in rather than supporting the local village services.

■ **Figure 2.34:** A shanty town in Brazil

Advances in communication and information technology such as email and faxes means many people can now work from home

Better environment: less pollution and congestion

People moving back to villages: **counterurbanisation**

People can commute to their jobs in towns and cities due to improved transport

Business parks are being built in rural areas generating employment opportunities away from the city

■ **Figure 2.35:** Reasons for counterurbanisation in Britain

Figure 2.36 shows the village of Thorpe Hesley near Sheffield which can also be seen on the OS map extract of Sheffield on page 60 at grid square 3796. Thorpe Hesley is a good example of a village that has become suburbanised. It is situated in a rural area but is only 9.5 km (6 miles) from Sheffield, hence people wishing to live in a more rural environment have left Sheffield and relocated there. Thorpe Hesley has grown significantly in the last thirty years and, although it maintains a typical village centre, it is surrounded by new sprawling housing estates. There are few

■ **Figure 2.36:** OS map extract of Thorpe Hesley

services in Thorpe Hesley as the majority of its population commute to Sheffield and use services such as those found at Meadowhall shopping centre at grid reference 393909.

Although most people living in Thorpe Hesley are commuters, two groups of people in particular may feel isolated in the village due to the lack of services. Elderly people may not have their own transport or may not be in good enough health to travel out of the village to perform vital tasks such as food shopping. Young people such as teenagers may also feel isolated and bored due to the lack of social opportunities in the village which has at times led to petty crime such as vandalism. Both groups may suffer from a feeling of lack of community as there is no social focus around facilities in the village due to their absence.

Exercise 2G

1 Write sentences to explain the meaning of each of the following words:

migration   **emigrate**   **immigrant**   **refugee**

2 Why do migrants sometimes have no choice about moving to a different area or country? Try to use example developing countries in your answer.

3 Why are people living in developed countries attracted to live abroad, whether temporarily or permanently?

4 Write sentences to explain the meaning of each of the following terms:

rural-urban migration   **counterurbanisation**

5 Draw two star diagrams to illustrate, firstly, the reasons why villages are becoming suburbanised and, secondly, the problems this may create.

Extension questions
6 Why do you think illegal immigrants risk going to prison in order to live in a country other than their own?

7 How has counterurbanisation affected the function of rural settlements today?

8 Look at the OS map extract of Sheffield on pages 60 and 61. Identify a village other than Thorpe Hesley that may have been suburbanised. How will this have affected different social groups in the community?

Exercise 2H: Enquiry suggestion

To determine whether shops in your nearest settlement are high or low order services, conduct a survey outside selected shops asking customers a series of questions. To start you will need to draw a map of the streets where you will be conducting the survey, for which you may need a local street map or town plan. Identify which shops you wish to stand outside and make predictions as to whether they will be selling convenience or comparison goods. Before you depart, design a questionnaire that will ask customers what they have bought, if they compared the price of the item they bought with prices in any other shop, how often they buy this item and how far they have travelled to buy it. You could add other questions to see which mode of transport they used and why. You will need to ask the permission of the shopkeepers to conduct surveys outside their shops and should conduct the survey with at least one other person. When you return, analyse your results to see if your predictions were correct. Finally, put the shops you have selected into a hierarchy.

Exercise 2I: Past exam questions

1 Many rural settlements are changing. Some are growing, others are declining. Using examples where possible, explain why this is. (6 marks)

2 Look at this sketch map (Figure 2.37) which shows where the different types of shopping centres are located in a town.

(a) Describe where each of the shopping areas is located. (4 marks)

(b) Suggest reasons why this pattern of shopping has developed in the town. (8 marks)

3 State two ways in which the urban land use pattern is different in a developed country from a developing country. (2 marks)

4 Look at the map of the town (Figure 2.38 on page 59) and describe its site. (2 marks)

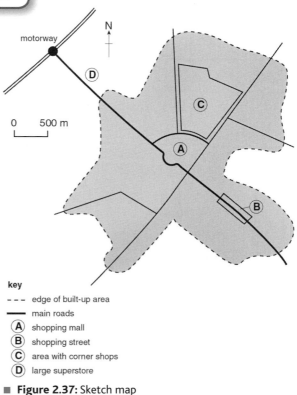

key

- - - edge of built-up area
—— main roads
(A) shopping mall
(B) shopping street
(C) area with corner shops
(D) large superstore

■ **Figure 2.37:** Sketch map

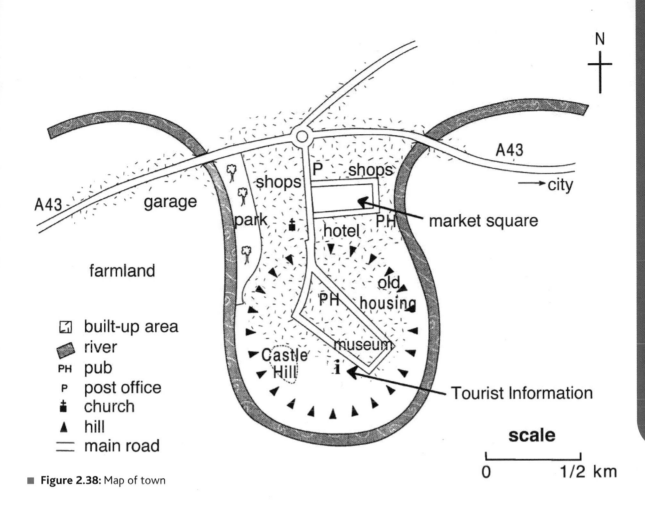

■ **Figure 2.38:** Map of town

Map labels: N, A43, city, A43, garage, shops, P, shops, market square, park, hotel, PH, farmland, old housing, PH, museum, Castle Hill, i, Tourist Information, scale, 0, 1/2 km

Key:
- built-up area
- river
- PH pub
- P post office
- church
- ▲ hill
- main road

5 Column A below shows services provided in various settlements. Put the
following settlements in the right place in column B: **village; city; town; hamlet**.

A	B
Department store, university, airport	
Few scattered houses, no shops	
Primary school, shop, post office	
Secondary school, library, bank	(4 marks)

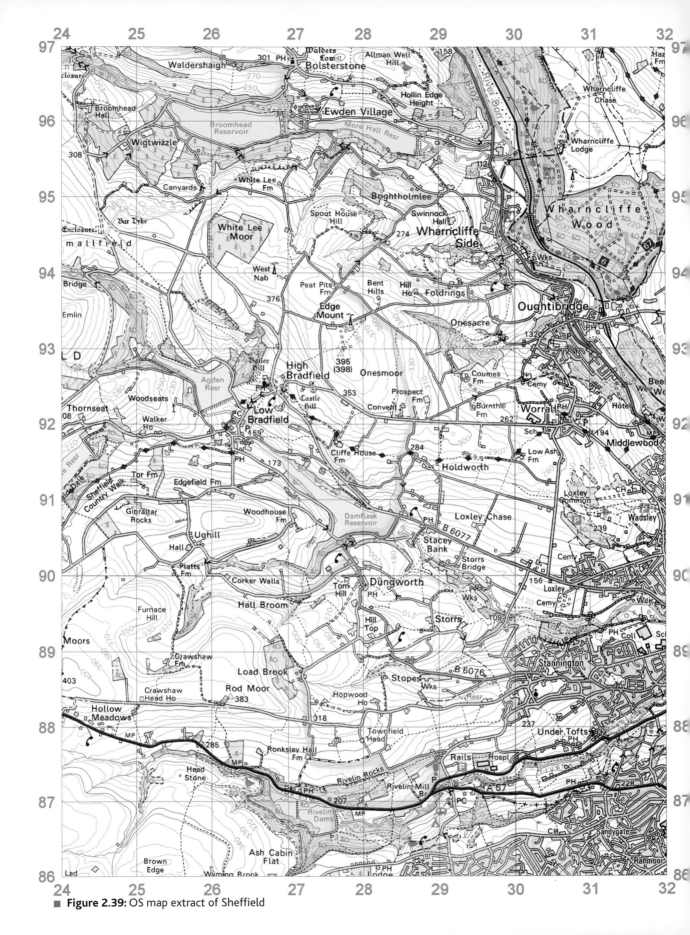

■ **Figure 2.39:** OS map extract of Sheffield

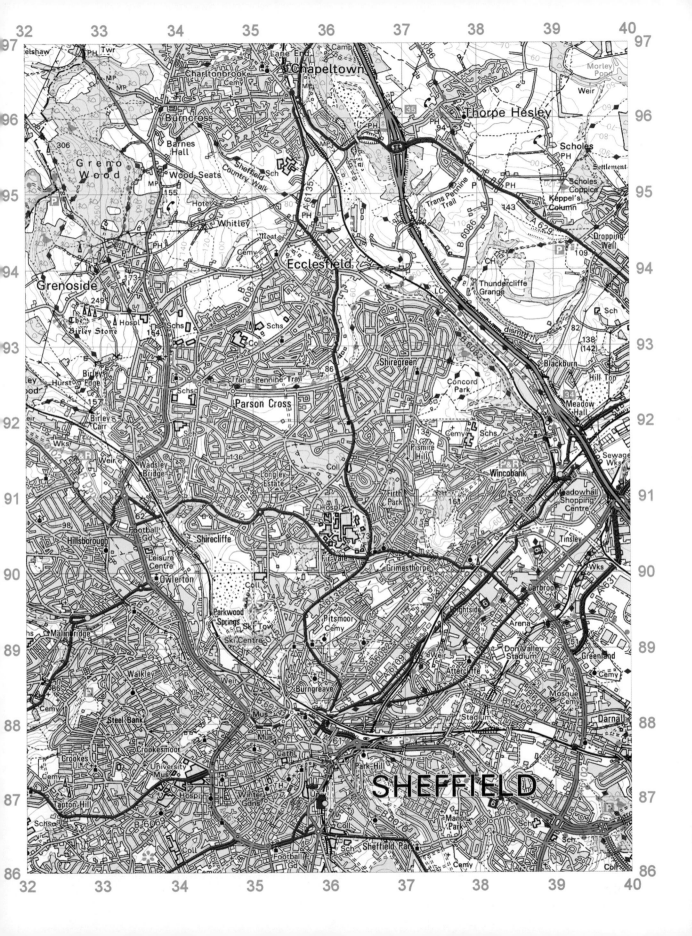

Exercise 2J: Scholarship or more advanced questions

(a) What is the difference between site and situation? (4 marks)

(b) How have rural settlements changed over the last fifty years? (6 marks)

(c) What effect have the changes had on life in rural areas? (9 marks)

(d) What is the future of rural areas? (6 marks)

Exercise 2K

1 Solve the following clues.

   (a) Someone who lives in one settlement but travels to work in another (8 letters)

   (b) Process of people moving either within or between countries (9 letters)

   (c) Type of informal housing found in developing countries (6 letters)

   (d) Opposite to question 8 (5 letters)

   (e) A type of housing often found in the outer suburbs of the city (8 letters)

   (f) An old building that has been redeveloped has been... (10 letters)

   (g) The purpose of a settlement (8 letters)

   (h) A built-up area – town or city (5 letters)

   (i) Name given to people who do not settle but move from place to place (7 letters)

   (j) Settlement pattern found along coasts and valleys (6 letters)

2 Make a list of all the key terms in this chapter and their definitions. Check your definitions against the glossary on page 160.

Transport and industry

In this chapter you will study:

- how we use different forms of transport to get around Britain
- the problems caused by the use of cars and one of the government's solutions in HS2
- how jobs are categorised into different groups
- what makes particular industries locate in certain places
- the globalisation of industry and its effect on developing countries
- the types of farming in Britain and where they are found
- what factors influence the location of a secondary industry
- why tourism is such a large global industry and how it influences Britain in a positive and negative way
- where Toyota and Jaguar manufacture their cars in Britain and how manufacturing in developing countries can go wrong, with a look at the Ranza Plaza factory collapse in Bangladesh.

3.1 Britain's transport networks

How do we get around?

Roads and cars

How did you get to school this morning? More than likely you came by car along a stretch of the 213 750 miles of roads in Britain. Figure 3.1 on page 65 clearly shows that most journeys are made by car, but why is this and what impact is this having on our environment?

The number of cars on Britain's roads has increased significantly over the past 50 years, with approximately 32 million cars on the roads today. This is because cars have become more affordable. In 1971 just eight per cent of households had two or more cars and nearly 50 per cent did not own a car. Today, over 30 per cent of households have two or more cars while the number of people without a car has halved. The car, compared with public transport, offers individuals greater freedom and flexibility of travel. Combine increased car ownership with the massive amount of road building which the government continues to invest in (alongside funding public transport) and the dominance of the car is no surprise. But what problems have all these new roads and more cars created?

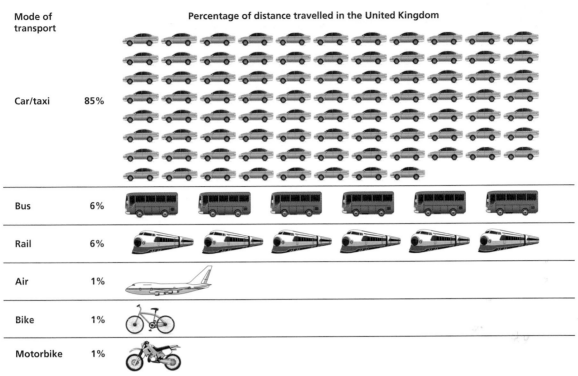

Mode of transport		Percentage of distance travelled in the United Kingdom
Car/taxi	85%	
Bus	6%	
Rail	6%	
Air	1%	
Bike	1%	
Motorbike	1%	

■ **Figure 3.1:** Transport methods we use to get around in the UK

Pollution
- Road transport accounts for 22 per cent of total UK emissions of carbon dioxide (CO_2), a major contributor to climate change.
- Noise from road traffic affects 30 per cent of people in the UK. Sources include engine noise, tyre noise, car horns, car stereos, door slamming, and squeaking brakes.

Losing the countryside
- Roughly 2 per cent of Britain's land is covered by roads.
- In total, local governments plan to spend £710 million from 2015 on new road capacity for cars and lorries.

Congestion
- New roads make journeys quicker in the short term, so people drive more often and even move farther from work where houses are cheaper.
- A major study looking into the impact of the Newbury bypass showed that traffic levels predicted for 2010 in Newbury were already reached in 2003 – and that traffic had increased by almost 50 per cent in that period, leading to congestion on a new road!

■ **Figure 3.2:** Traffic jams on the M25

There are several ways in which congestion can be reduced. Bypasses can be built around heavily congested towns or cities, but this involves building roads over open countryside. Applying heavy charges for car owners to park in these settlements may reduce congestion, but may also reduce the number of people visiting the settlement and using its businesses. A solution to congestion and the pollution it creates in cities is to introduce a Congestion Charge Zone, such as the one introduced in London in 2003. Look at the fact file below, focusing on London's congestion zone, and consider who benefits from it and who might be disadvantaged by it.

The large department store John Lewis reported a 7.3 per cent fall in sales at its central London Oxford Street store within six months of the Congestion Charge Zone being introduced. In the same period, sales at John Lewis' other stores in the Greater London area, which were located outside the Congestion Charge Zone, actually increased by 1.7 per cent.

Between the start of the congestion charge (in 2003) and 2007 CO_2 emissions were reduced by 20 per cent, improving the air quality for the residents and people who work within the Congestion Charge Zone.

■ **Figure 3.3:** Congestion charges

The average number of cars and delivery vehicles entering the central zone is roughly 60 000 fewer than before the congestion charge was applied. Around 50–60 per cent of this reduction is because people are using public transport instead.

With a current charge of £10 a day for a vehicle to enter the Congestion Zone, and fines of £60 (rising to £187 if not paid on time), the Congestion Charge Zone has been criticised as simply being a scheme for the government to make money. The government receives approximately £250 million a year in revenue from the congestion charge.

'We are destroying the habitats of wildlife by building more and more roads on greenfield sites. Central and local governments should invest further in schemes which encourage people to use cycles.'

'I rely on the train to get me into the city but would like it to be quicker.'

'A recent study has proven a link between heart disease and noise levels from living near an airport. I don't think the speed and convenience of air travel is more important than people's health and I'm against airport expansion.'

'I live in the countryside and have to rely on my parents to drive me to see my friends; there should be better bus services for young people.'

Look at the opinions of the different people in Figure 3.4 and ask yourself:

● Which groups of people think we need to build more roads?
● Do people think of themselves or the environment when they talk about transport?
● Which groups do you think are going to be happy with transport systems in 20 years time?
● What do you think people you know in your local area would think about transport development?

'My local village was becoming congested and polluted until they built a new bypass; now it is much better.'

■ **Figure 3.4:** Differing opinions about the need to build more roads

Driving the economy

It is easy to think of all the problems that cars and road building cause, but have you thought about what the car does for our **economy**?

- Britain's car manufacturing sector has a turnover of over £52 billion, making around 1.5 million passenger vehicles and 200 000 commercial vehicles each year.
- Around 180 000 people are directly employed in car manufacturing in Britain, with a further 640 000 people employed in car supply, sales and servicing.
- Britain is a major centre for engine manufacturing and around 3 million engines are produced in the country each year.
- Recent figures suggest the amount of goods moved in Britain totals 139 billion tons per annum.
- In the 2011 census, driving was the most common form of transport for **commuting** to work, used by 15.3 million people (57.5 per cent of the working population).
- Add to this the thousands of jobs created in Britain from road construction and maintenance and the economic importance of the car cannot be ignored.

Alternatives to cars and roads

What are the alternatives?

Roads are just one possible <u>routeway</u> and cars are just one form of transport. Let's have a look at the alternatives.

Buses

Buses are the most frequently used form of public transport. Day in and day out they link thousands of people up and down the country to jobs, schools and shops. However, government spending cuts are currently contributing to local councils increasing bus fares and reducing the number of routes they operate.

Buses do not offer the freedom and flexibility of the car, but think about the amount of pollution and congestion they reduce. A full bus can carry up to 70 people, who each might have used a car if a bus was not available. There are many bus routes and many buses in urban areas, but travelling by bus is not as easy for those living in rural areas, as these areas tend to have fewer routes and less frequent services.

■ **Figure 3.5:** The London bus

Trains

The National Rail network in Britain covers over 10 000 miles, has 189 routes and carries over 18 000 passenger trains a day. Once nationally owned under British Rail, there are now 25 different train operators offering services. The railway network in Britain is also used to transport **freight** with over a 1000 freight trains operating daily, often transporting heavy <u>raw materials</u> across the country. In 1994 the Channel Tunnel was opened, linking Britain with mainland Europe. The government is presently considering whether to invest further in railways, with the proposed High Speed 2 (<u>HS2</u>) rail project – see page 72.

■ **Figure 3.6:** A high speed train

Trains are often quicker than cars and when travelling longer distances within Britain are usually cheaper than planes. However, like buses, trains cannot compete with cars in terms of flexibility, and ticket prices continue to rise at a rate that is making the train unaffordable for many. Trains also tend to serve passengers seeking transport between urban areas better than passengers needing transport to and from rural areas.

Ferries and boats

Not many of you will come to school by boat, but when a stretch of water needs to be crossed invariably a ferry service of some nature will be in operation. In London the Woolwich Ferry links the North and South circular roads. Gosport and Portsmouth are linked by the Gosport Ferry, and Southampton and the Isle of Wight are linked by ferry and fast Catamaran ferries. In addition, waterbuses operate on rivers in some of the country's largest cities such as London, Cardiff and Bristol. Although we now have the Channel Tunnel, you may well have started a holiday in Europe by crossing the channel by ferry from Portsmouth, Dover or Folkestone.

Britain also has over 2000 miles of canals, constructed during the Industrial Revolution to transport raw materials and goods throughout the country. Today Britain's ports are essential entrance and exit points for goods being imported or exported. <u>Containerisation</u>, the use of large metal containers to stow and transport goods across the world on container ships, has meant many small ports have become unusable as they are too shallow or too small to accommodate container ships. Approximately 95 per

■ **Figure 3.7:** The Woolwich ferry

cent of freight now enters Britain by sea through large container ship ports such as Southampton and Felixstowe.

Air

Travelling within Britain by air is certainly not the cheapest form of transport, and, unless you are hiring a private jet, is limited to a relatively small amount of routes between regional airports. However, the cost of flying has dropped dramatically over the last 30 years with the arrival of low cost airlines, such as easyJet and Ryanair, making

■ **Figure 3.8:** An easyJet airplane taking off from Gatwick Airport

flying popular not only with tourists but business people looking to save time. The demand for passenger air travel is forecast to increase from the current level of 236 million passengers to 465 million in 2030. London Heathrow Airport is amongst the top ten busiest airports in the world, and more than half of all passengers travelling by air in the UK currently travel via the five London area airports.

However, the impact of increased popularity of air travel is damaging our environment. Whilst carbon emissions from all UK activities other than air travel declined by 9 per cent in the last decade, carbon emissions from planes doubled in the same period. Add to this the **noise pollution** of planes and the congestion created on roads around airports, and we should think carefully about how and where we build airports in Britain.

Geography in the news

Think about what transport developments or problems are occurring at the moment in your local area. Perhaps a bypass is being planned near your town or village, or maybe your part of the city needs more cycle lanes. More than likely your local area will suffer from congestion and need more car parking space. Local transport issues are usually reported in your local newspapers and magazines. Take a look at the articles in the free papers and magazines you get through the door, and see if you pick up on any transport news that might be occurring in your local area and which might affect you and your family. Also have a look at the 'In your area' part of website below, to see if any of the campaigns are in your local area!

● www.bettertransport.org.uk

Exercise 3A

1 Why is the car the most popular form of transport in Britain?

2 Draw a spider diagram with a picture of a car in the middle and the caption *Environmental problems*. Now add legs to the spider diagram with facts about the environmental problems cars create in Britain.

3 In what ways is the car important to Britain's economy?

4 Imagine you are the Mayor of London! You are campaigning for re-election and are preparing for a radio interview, in which you know the interviewer will ask you about the congestion charge. Prepare a list of reasons why you feel the Congestion Charge Zone should either be extended or scrapped.

5 Choose one of the four main alternatives to the car (plane/train/bus/boat) and set out three reasons why you think the government should invest further in this form of transport.

Extension questions

6 'However much the government invests in public transport, people will continue to use cars and demand more road building.' Write 300 words discussing your views on this statement.

7 Is there a transport solution that we are missing? Are other countries with similar road congestion problems investing in anything other than buses and trains? What is *monorail*? Investigate and write up to 300 words.

3.2 HS2 rail proposal

An investment for the future or a waste of money?

You might have heard debate in the news about the government's proposal to build a high speed rail link between London and Birmingham and beyond. In fact, closer inspection of Figure 3.9 shows that there are two clear phases of the project. Phase one of the line is between London and Birmingham, with construction planned to begin in 2017 and be completed by 2026. Phase two extends high speed rail travel to other major economic centres in the north of Britain, and is projected to be completed by 2032. The HS2 project is not in fact an idea created by the present government, but was developed in 2009 following the success of HS1 which links central London with the Channel Tunnel and the rest of mainland Europe's high speed railway network.

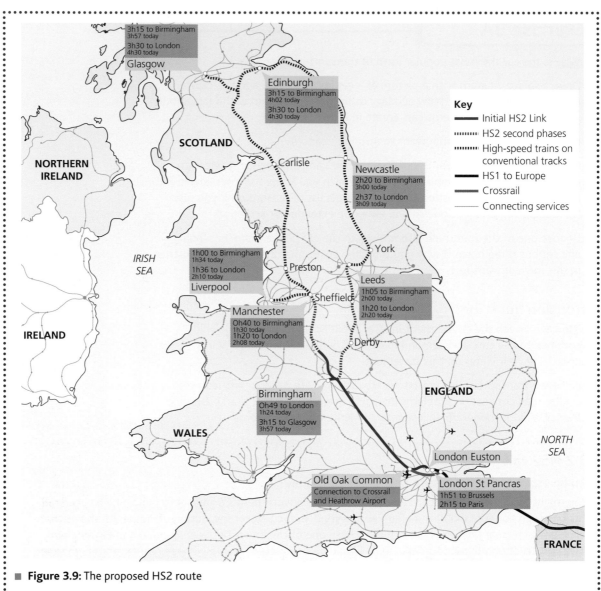

Figure 3.9: The proposed HS2 route

With a price tag of over £42 billion and unavoidable damage to the environment, HS2 was always going to attract significant opposition at a local and national scale. Look at Figure 3.10 and think about which side of the railway fence you sit on – supporting HS2 or opposing it?

■ **Figure 3.10:** Which side of the railway fence do you sit on?

Opposing

● Other possible solutions exist, such as increasing the length of trains on existing routes.
● Some argue that only particular groups of people will directly benefit from HS2, namely commuters who travel between major cities.
● With ever increasing numbers of workers now working from home using the internet to communicate with colleagues and clients, those in opposition of HS2 question the true benefit of improved speed of train journeys.
● Loss of open countryside and wildlife <u>habitat</u>, as the new line cuts through environmentally sensitive areas such as the Chilterns.

Supporting

● The road network is congested and nearing its capacity. Providing high speed rail will reduce traffic congestion in our city centres as more people will be attracted to taking the faster train services. Hence HS2 will not only mean train travellers receive a faster service but also that our city centres will have less traffic congestion, as commuters opt for the train over the car.
● Many badly needed jobs will be created, not only in the building of HS2 but also in its operation.
● Trains have a better safety record than the roads. Recent passenger death rates by car were 1.9 per billion km and by train were 0.3 per billion km.
● The cost of construction will be spread out over 15–20 years; therefore we can afford it.

At first glance, most people would think that the high cost of constructing HS2 might not be worth it. However, as the points on the 'railway side' of the fence in Figure 3.10 show, the government believes this is not true in the long term. Rather than focusing on the cost, the media has picked up on local protest groups who are taking action to raise attention to the negative impact of HS2 on their local area. No rural community wants a potentially noisy and ugly rail line running through their countryside, even if it is going to benefit the nation economically. NIMBY (**n**ot **i**n **m**y **b**ack **y**ard) stories are easy for the media to report on and have filled newspapers since proposals for HS2 were confirmed by the government. Visit the websites of newspapers such as the *Daily Mail* (www.dailymail.co.uk) and search for articles using the keywords 'HS2' or 'high speed rail link' – you are bound to find articles which report strong rural opposition to the route of HS2.

1 If all parts of HS2 are constructed, how long will the following journeys take?

- Birmingham to London
- Manchester to London
- Leeds to Paris (allowing 40 minutes for transfer in London)

2 Draw a train with three carriages. In each carriage describe an advantage of HS2.

3 Now draw another train with three carriages. This time in each carriage describe a problem which HS2 might cause.

4 £42 billion is a lot of money. Which other form of transport do you think the money could be spent on instead? Explain your choice and describe the benefits your choice would bring the public.

Extension question

5 Look at Figure 3.11. Imagine you live in Baldwin's Gate or Whitmore Heath. Write a letter of approximately 300 words to your local MP outlining why you object to the plans and the impact the HS2 will have on your local community.

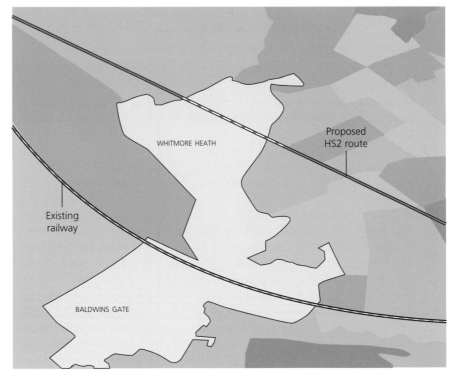

■ **Figure 3.11:** Proposed HS2 route past Baldwin's Gate and Whitmore Heath

3.3 Putting jobs into different categories

The employment structure

A country with a successful economy has a large proportion of its population in employment in a wide range of jobs within a great number of economic activities. These economic activities are classified into four categories according to their stage in the process of production.

Primary activities

Jobs in a primary activity are involved in extracting raw materials directly from the earth or sea. There are five main **primary activities**: farming, fishing (see Figure 3.12), forestry, mining, and oil and natural gas drilling. These industries employ millions of people worldwide and are the economic activities that formed the foundation of ancient economies. These activities are still a vital part of modern economies, but in some developed countries **sunset industries** are declining due to cheap imports of raw materials from developing countries.

■ **Figure 3.12:** Primary activity – fishing

Secondary activities

People employed in **secondary activities** use the raw materials produced by the primary industries to manufacture a product. Manufacturing usually takes place in a factory (see Figure 3.13), which could be located on a **business park**. The products that are made include electrical items, cars, furniture and clothes and include industries such as oil refining and food processing or packaging.

■ **Figure 3.13:** Secondary activity – cheese factory

Tertiary activities

Those employed in **tertiary activities** sell or **retail** products manufactured by secondary industries to the public in shops such as supermarkets, department stores and high street chain stores. Tertiary workers can also provide services to the public, including free services such as the police, fire or health service, or private services such as entertainment, tourism or finance.

Quaternary activities

The role of those employed in **quaternary activities** is to research and develop new products, often for **sunrise industries** producing **hi-tech goods** such as computers and mobile phones. Scientists

■ **Figure 3.14:** Tertiary activity – firefighter

■ **Figure 3.15:** Quaternary activity – a chemist working in a laboratory

researching products such as medicines are another example of people working in a quaternary activity (see Figure 3.15). The information industries and consultancy are also sometimes included in this category.

Identifying economic activities on OS maps

It is necessary to be able to identify different economic activities on OS maps.

Farms, woodland plantations and quarries or mines are good examples of common primary activities to be found on an OS map, as shown in Figure 3.16.

■ **Figure 3.16:** Primary activities

■ **Figure 3.17:** Secondary activities

Secondary activities (industries) are indicated by *industrial estate* (or sometimes *ind estate*), *factory* or *wks* (short for *works*), as shown in Figure 3.17.

The easiest type of industry to find examples of on OS maps is tertiary industry, as shown in Figure 3.18. Maps that show settlements will include examples of services such as hospitals, schools, train stations, sports centres, post offices, public houses, etc.

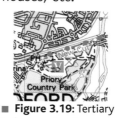

■ **Figure 3.18:** Tertiary industry – hospital

■ **Figure 3.19:** Tertiary industry – tourism

Tourist attractions and facilities are often coloured blue on OS maps, as shown on Figure 3.19. Tourism is an important tertiary industry.

Use the map of Bedford in Figure 3.20 on page 77 to identify different examples of primary, secondary and tertiary industries.

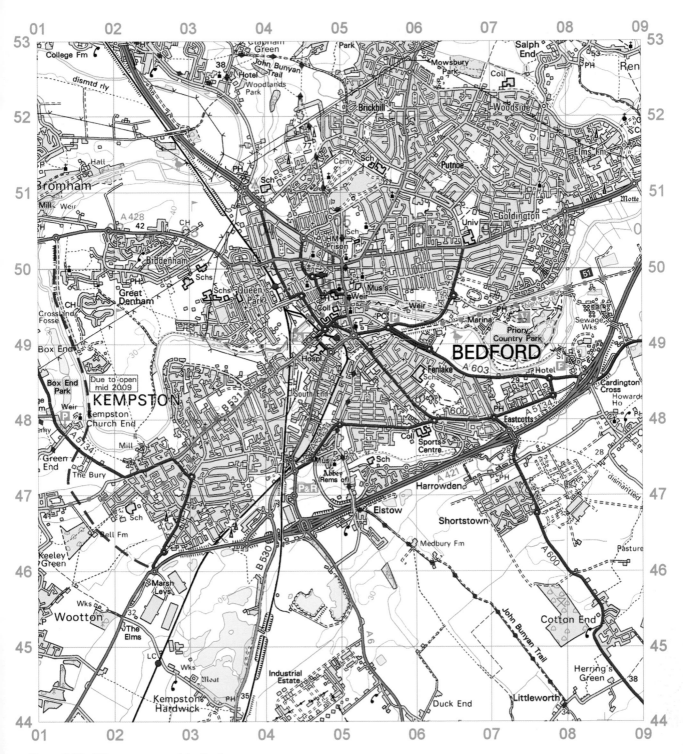

■ **Figure 3.20:** OS map extract of Bedford

Employment structures in developed countries and developing countries

If you conducted a survey in your class to discover how parents were employed, it would probably reveal that many of them were employed in tertiary industry (bankers, lawyers, doctors). Britain has a very high proportion of its population employed in this sector because it is a wealthy developed country the population of which can afford public services (healthcare, education, police) and private services (shops, financial services, entertainment), all of which are catered for by tertiary industries.

In developing countries there tend to be lower levels of employment overall, and a higher proportion of employment in primary and secondary industries. Due to fewer education facilities in developing countries the majority of the population may not possess the skills required for employment in tertiary industries. As the population is poor, it is less able to afford tertiary products and services, resulting in a reduced market for these services.

Location of industries

Over the last two centuries industries such as steel and iron manufacture, and mills (paper and woollen), often grew up around the source of their raw materials. For example, paper mills were found near a source of wood, and woollen mills near big sheep farming areas. Steel manufacturers were found near coal fields (for their power supply).

However, things have changed and many industries in Britain today are much freer to locate wherever they like. The traditional need to be close to raw materials, energy supply and the market is no longer as important. With greatly improved transport and communication now available, the two most important factors of location have become access and transport hubs, for example ports, railway terminals and airports, and the cost of labour. Industries can now search the world to find the lowest cost of labour.

Sometimes people say 'the world is getting smaller' or describe the world as a 'global village'.

The increase in trade and the sharing of ideas and cultures throughout the world is called globalisation. This has been made possible by improvements in transport and communications. Some companies have taken advantage of these improvements to move their operations to different parts of the world where there are favourable location factors (such as low labour costs). These companies are called TNCs and are often large, wealthy and powerful organisations.

The location of TNCs in a developing country can have a significant effect on the people and the country's economy. Some of these effects are positive:

- A reduction in trade taxes means that companies in developing countries find it easier to trade their products with other developing countries and more recently with developed countries.
- Huge improvements in transport and demand for global holiday destinations from people in developed countries means that many developing countries are now generating a high income from tourism. For example, many Asian and African countries such as Thailand and Egypt generate money from tourists through a tourist tax paid to the government which then invests the money in developing facilities such as schools, roads and hospitals.
- Many TNCs that decide to locate their factories in developing countries provide jobs for local people who may otherwise be unemployed.

However, globalisation also has disadvantages:

- Governments in developing countries have often encouraged the growth of industry without considering the environmental effects. China, for example, contains 16 out of the 20 most polluted cities in the world.
- Some TNCs have located their factories in developing countries in order to **exploit** the low wages in these countries and thereby increase their profits. Often factory workers are paid below the average wage of workers in developed countries, and forced to work very long hours in poor conditions where they may not have access to drinking water (see Figure 3.21). In some factories child labour is used, even when it is illegal.
- The rapid increase in TNCs locating their factories in developing countries means that many developing countries are becoming dependent on these companies for jobs. Many local people, who may have previously worked for local companies or as farmers, take jobs with TNCs.

■ **Figure 3.21:** Poor conditions in a factory in a developing country

Exercise 3C

1 Create four list headings as below:

Primary **Secondary** **Tertiary** **Quaternary**

Now list the following jobs under the correct headings:

Firefighter	Car assembly worker	Inventor
Farmer	Oil drill operator	Builder
Lawyer	Professional footballer	Dentist
Research scientist	Textile factory worker	

2 The following phrases all relate to the oil industry in Britain. Match them up to the correct type of industry: primary, secondary, tertiary or quaternary.

(a) Researching new, more environmentally friendly fuels

(b) Drilling for oil in the North Sea

(c) Refining oil at processing plants on the east coast of Scotland to create petrol and other by-products

(d) Selling petrol at petrol stations throughout Britain and Europe

3 Look at the map of Bedford in Figure 3.20 on page 77. For each of the following types of industry, find an example, name the example and give a six figure grid reference for the example you have identified.

(a) Primary industry

(b) Secondary industry

(c) Tertiary industry

4 List examples of primary, secondary and tertiary industries in your local area. You may need to look at a local map or conduct some research on the internet to help you answer this question.

5 (a) What does the term 'globalisation' mean?

(b) List two positive effects of globalisation on developing countries and two negative effects.

Extension question

6 Why do transnational companies (TNCs) often locate their manufacturing sectors in developing countries?

◯ 3.4 Examples of primary, secondary and tertiary activities (industries)

Farming: A primary industry

Around 10 000 years ago humans developed the skills to grow crops from seeds and breed animals. The primary industry of farming, or agriculture, was born. The different types of farming can be split into three groups: arable, pastoral and mixed.

- **Arable farming** involves growing crops such as barley, wheat and oilseed rape. Arable farming also includes **market gardening**, which involves growing fruit and vegetables, often on a small scale and sometimes in controlled greenhouse conditions.
- Pastoral farming involves breeding or rearing animals for their meat or other produce. Sheep, cows, pigs, chickens and turkeys are all bred for their meat. Poultry (chickens and turkeys) are also reared to produce eggs, and cows are often bred for their milk (dairy farming).

- **Mixed farming** is the use of a single farm for multiple purposes, for example arable and pastoral farming. Mixed farming on a small scale, **subsistence agriculture**, is common in parts of Africa, Asia and South America. This is a method of farming in which farmers plan to grow only enough food to feed the family, pay taxes or other dues, and perhaps provide a small surplus to sell.

Figure 3.22 shows that most pastoral farming in Britain is located in the north-west and most arable farming in the south-east. This is a generalised map. In reality, the <u>distribution</u> of farming types is much more complex.

Physical factors that influence a farmer

The distribution of farming types as shown in Figure 3.22 is due to the **physical factors** that influence the type of farming that is appropriate in a particular region. These factors are: relief, soil, temperature and rainfall.

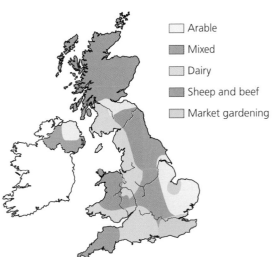

■ **Figure 3.22:** Map of Britain showing the general distribution of farming types

Relief
The relief aspects of the land (its shape and height) affect what type of farming is chosen. Flat land is suitable for arable farming as machinery can be used on it. Steep land is better for pastoral sheep farming because sheep can graze on steep slopes.

Soil
The depth and quality of soil have an effect on the type of farming. If the soil is deep and **fertile** it will be more suitable for arable farming, if shallow and lacking in fertility it may be better for pastoral or mixed farming.

Temperature
The temperature of a local area affects the type of farming. Some crops are damaged by freezing temperatures; therefore colder, highland areas may not be as suitable for arable farming as warmer lowland areas.

Rainfall
The amount of rainfall an area receives is a crucial physical factor. Although both animals and crops need water, too much rainfall can destroy crops by encouraging disease or causing flooding.

Pastoral farming is more common in the north and north-west of Britain where land is steeper, soils are thinner, and the climate is often colder and wetter. The south and east of Britain is flatter, the soils tend to be deeper and richer and the climate is warmer and drier, so there tends to be more arable farming, particularly cereal crops.

Human factors that influence a farmer

The type of farming that a farmer chooses to practise and the exact location of a farm may also be influenced by **human factors**: farm size, technology, accessibility to the market and government help.

Farm size

The size of a farm is an important factor. Pastoral farming requires a large amount of land for the animals to graze on. By contrast, arable farmers can sow crops densely in a small area and practise **intensive farming**.

Technology

The amount of technology used on a farm varies according to the type of farming. Arable farms tend to be farmed intensively, so a great deal of money is spent on fertilisers and special machinery such as combine harvesters (see Figure 3.23). Pastoral farmers tend to practise **extensive farming** with less money spent on machinery.

■ **Figure 3.23:** Arable farming often means spending money on special machinery

Accessibility to the market

A farm's profit will be dependent on how close the farm is to its market. It is beneficial for a farm to be close and well linked by roads and motorways to a big market. Farms that produce **perishable goods** (items that go bad quickly such as fruit and milk) need to be located close to their markets.

Government help

A government can encourage certain types of farming if it feels there is market demand. For example, dairy farmers are given **grants** and **subsidies** (financial assistance to guarantee a minimum income). Farmers may adopt a particular type of farming if government grants make it more profitable.

Extension topic: The history of farming in Britain

From the beginning of agriculture, thousands of years ago, until quite recently, only minor changes in farming methods were developed. In many developing countries, farming is still carried on in the same way as it was hundreds of years ago. However, in Britain and other developed countries during the mid to latter part of the 20th century, farming changed significantly with the development of machinery, pesticides and fertilisers. Farms have become more commercial as they have merged to form fewer but larger farms.

Since the middle of the 20th century farmers have found it more difficult to stay in business due to competition from foreign producers. Today the **European Union (EU)**, along with the British government, helps different groups of farmers to stay in business by providing them with grants and subsidies. This support for farmers has, in the past, created overproduction of agricultural produce within Britain and other European countries. Surpluses were produced. To overcome this waste, farmers are now given **quotas** limiting the amount of produce, such as milk, they can sell within the EU. **Diversification** has also been encouraged (where farmers change what they use their land for) and land can be left **fallow** (idle or uncultivated) for a number of years.

In order to diversify, some farmers have sold parts of their land to be developed for housing or industry. Many farmers have chosen to keep the land, as it may become more economical to cultivate in future. Others have developed income-generating activities such as golf courses, riding schools, paintballing centres and campsites.

Secondary industries

Location factors for secondary industry

There is a huge variety of secondary industries manufacturing or processing all sorts of goods, from ships to clothes to electronic items. This variety means that many different location factors can influence where a factory is situated, including: raw materials, site proximity to market, labour supply, power source and transport links.

Raw materials

Some secondary industries manufacture products that are made from heavy raw materials which are difficult or expensive to transport; for example, a masonry factory or a paper mill (see Figure 3.24). Others use raw materials that are perishable, such as food in food processing factories. In both cases these secondary industries are ideally located close to the raw materials they use.

■ **Figure 3.24:** Paper mill

The site

All secondary industries look for the best value site for their factory, whether it is a small unit on an industrial estate or a factory that covers a huge area. Generally, land is cheaper the further north you travel within Britain and, on a local scale, land tends to be cheaper the further you travel away from city centres.

Flat ground is the best option for the site of a factory as it is much more expensive to build on uneven or steep land.

Proximity to the market

It is valuable for some secondary industries to be close to their market. This reduces the transport costs of sending goods to market and is useful when it is necessary to deliver goods quickly. Newspaper printers tend to be located in major cities so their newspapers can be quickly and easily distributed to the majority of their customers (see Figure 3.25). Assembly industries, such as car manufacturing, are also often located near their markets or close to good transport routes.

■ **Figure 3.25:** Newspaper press, Canary Wharf, London

Labour supply

If a factory requires many manual workers to operate machinery it is better for it to be located near a large urban area which can supply the workers (labour). Indeed a company may choose to locate its factory in a certain country because there is a good supply of labour there.

Modern manufacturing industries producing hi-tech goods such as computers and mobile phones, or specialist secondary industries such as aircraft assembly may need a small but more skilled labour force. These industries tend to locate near cities with universities where such skilled workers can be more easily recruited.

Power source

Many early industries grew up in locations near fast-flowing rivers, and used their power to run machinery (see Figure 3.26). The **textile industry** positioned its mills on the highland rivers of Yorkshire and Lancashire during the 19th century to take advantage of this natural power source. Many of these mills have now been converted into modern housing or offices and some are museums celebrating this period of Britain's industrial history.

■ **Figure 3.26:** Cromford Mill, Peak District, Derbyshire

Power is rarely a consideration for industry in Britain today since electricity is accessible through the **national grid** in all but the most remote of locations.

Transport links

The ability to transport manufactured goods to their various markets is an important location factor. Traditionally goods were transported by canal, rail or sea, therefore locations near these facilities were popular. Today most goods that are sold in Europe are transported by road, so being near a motorway junction is more important.

Extension topic: Why are location factors changing with time?

During the Industrial Revolution industry grew around power sources such as rivers and raw materials such as coal. Other industries then developed in these locations giving rise to the growth in urban areas that cover large areas of the UK today. In the last 30 years the world has experienced a new revolution that has changed the location factors that influence many secondary industries. The technological revolution, generated from the invention of the microchip, has led to the manufacture of hi-tech goods such as mobile phones and computers, that are very small, easily transported and sold on a global market.

Hi-tech firms are often referred to as **footloose** (they are not tied to one particular location). For example, they do not need to be near to a supply of heavy raw materials. In order for hi-tech firms, such as Microsoft, Nokia and Apple, to continue to develop new technologies and products, they prefer to locate near universities with which they can work on new product development. The National Grid for electricity has enabled those firms to locate far away from fixed power sources.

Hi-tech firms also cluster in order to share ideas and can often be found together on <u>science parks</u>. (Figure 3.27) These are purpose-built developments of industrial units and offices located on sites with some or all of the following advantages:

- good access: motorway junction, mainline train station nearby, airport within 50 kilometres (30 miles)
- newly built, high quality industrial units/offices
- landscaped grounds and gardens
- leisure facilities: sports centre, golf course, etc.
- room for expansion
- university nearby
- large car parking facilities.

■ **Figure 3.27:** Science park

Tertiary industries

Extension topic: The growth of tourism

The dictionary defines a tourist as 'a person who travels for pleasure' and tourism as 'the business of organising and providing services for tourists'. The World Tourism Organization (WTO) has further defined tourists as 'visitors who stay in the country visited for at least one night'. Today tourism is one of the world's largest tertiary industries employing millions of people in both developed countries and developing countries. The WTO estimated that, in 2008, 922 million tourist visits were made, generating US$944 billion.

Tourism really began in the 19th century when wealthy aristocrats were encouraged to make the Grand Tour, a cultural exploration of the major European cities. During the period of the Industrial Revolution, factory workers were allowed only a few days' holiday a year, usually in the summer, when they would travel to British coastal resorts such as Blackpool (see Figure 3.28). However, it was not until the second half of the 20th century that overseas tourism became an affordable opportunity for the average person in Britain.

During the 1970s mass tourism began as **package holidays** to European destinations such as Spain and Greece were sold. Rapid growth in tourism has continued (see Figure 3.29, page 87) due to improvements in transport such as the construction of the Channel Tunnel, as well as the availability and affordability of low cost airline flights within, and beyond, Europe.

■ **Figure 3.28:** Blackpool on a busy day

Despite catastrophes such as the 11th September 2001 terrorist attacks on the USA, and the Indian Ocean tsunami on 26th December 2004, the number of tourists continues to rise. This provides great benefits for many people but also causes problems for local people and their environment.

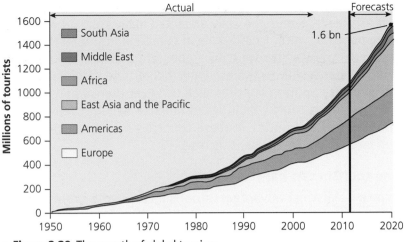

■ **Figure 3.29:** The growth of global tourism

How tourism can benefit an area

Tourism can be one of the most profitable tertiary industries. All tourists stay at least one night in their chosen holiday destination and therefore spend money at a hotel, bed and breakfast or campsite. Tourists also spend in other ways within the area they are visiting, including at restaurants, local attractions or on organised tours (see Figure 3.30). As well as bringing money and jobs to an area, tourists can also bring improved infrastructure. This benefits local people who can use the facilities that are built to attract tourists, for example, new roads and airports, leisure activities (for example, health centres and golf courses), new shopping centres and entertainment facilities. In developing countries many villages that previously lacked drainage, electricity and fresh water supplies now have them as a result of infrastructure developments for tourists.

■ **Figure 3.30:** Making money from tourists

How tourism benefits a country's economy

All companies involved in tourism (airlines, hotel chains, travel agents and so on) have to pay taxes on their profits to the government. In this way the economy of a country benefits from money generated by tourism. The money can then be invested in education, healthcare and other services, as well as developing existing and new tourist resorts. Some places may also apply a small percentage tourist tax to tourist accommodation or charge tourists for entering or departing their country.

Many developing countries remain poor because there is not enough employment for the increasing population. However, tourism can benefit these economies by reducing unemployment.

In the second half of the 20th century southern European countries such as Greece, Spain and Italy attracted many tourists with their sandy beaches, warm Mediterranean climate and interesting culture. These countries, which were once poor, are now wealthy developed countries partly due to the economic benefits tourism has brought. More recently poorer countries such as Egypt, Kenya and Thailand have developed tourist facilities in order to benefit their economies. However, political unrest in these countries has, at times, damaged tourism and the consequent income.

How tourism can harm an area

Despite its distinct advantages, tourism can create problems for the local environment and also present difficulties for local residents.

Environmental problems
Many tourists ultimately arrive at a tourist destination in cars or tourist buses which emit carbon dioxide causing air pollution and staining local historic buildings. Aeroplanes, which bring tourists from other countries, are also highly polluting.

■ **Figure 3.31:** Torremolinos, Costa del Sol, Spain

In the rush to make money from tourism, countries do not always carefully plan tourist developments. The beautiful landscape that attracted tourists can often be spoilt (visual pollution). A good example of this is the Costa del Sol in Spain, which has been covered in rows of apartment blocks (see Figure 3.31).

Fortunately, awareness of the negative environmental impact tourism can have is increasing. Eco-tourism sells itself on its minimal impact on the landscape and resources. This sunrise industry will continue to grow as wealthier westerners, who form the main global tourism market, seek holidays in low rise environmentally sensitive resorts and projects.

Even sections of land that were once wildlife habitats have been developed. The loss of habitat drives away animals, and birds no longer migrate there to breed. Large numbers of visitors to sensitive habitats can sometimes scare away the very animals they have come to see.

Increasingly, tourists are more considerate about the environment in which they are staying and have come to enjoy. However, littering remains a problem, especially in the larger tourist centres. Discarded tin cans and plastic items present a danger to wildlife and take hundreds if not thousands of years to biodegrade (the process by which organic materials are broken down by living organisms).

Problems for local residents

In some developing countries private land or land belonging to local communities has been used for tourist facilities and accommodation. Local people have been forced out of their homes or have lost their only form of income when farmland has been used for tourism.

In Britain many tourist centres are small towns or villages located in beautiful countryside. Although these areas may make money from tourism, they can also suffer from overcrowding in the height of summer. Narrow roads become congested with the volume of traffic that tourism brings (see Figure 3.32).

Because many tourist destinations are attractive places to live, people from other areas often buy holiday homes there. This can have two effects:

■ **Figure 3.32:** Traffic congestion in the pretty Cotswold village of Burford, Oxfordshire

● Prices increase to such a high level that local people struggle to buy houses in their local community.

● Because many of the holiday houses or flats are not occupied for most of the year, such places tend to lose their sense of community. Over time local shops and services may close down because the income from **seasonal jobs** is not sufficient.

In many European countries, small coastal villages have grown into large tourist centres with many bars and nightclubs catering for young people on holiday. Local residents often suffer the consequences of noise pollution and petty crime. In many overseas tourist resorts the local culture has changed too. In some areas the influence of English-speaking tourists has meant that locals often speak English more than they speak their own language (see Figure 3.33).

■ **Figure 3.33:** Nightlife in Ibiza

Exercise 3D

1 (a) Describe the distribution of farming types in Britain. You may wish to add a simple annotated sketch of Britain with your answer.

   (b) Explain the pattern you have described in part (a) by linking the distribution of farming types with different physical factors.

2 Explain the meaning of each of the following terms:

intensive farming   **extensive farming**
surplus   **subsistence agriculture**

3 Match the following secondary industries with the following location factors:

Location factor	**Industry**
Close to raw materials	Computer software development
Near a skilled labour supply	Fruit and vegetable growing
Close to the market	Large car manufacturing plant
Large and flat site for a factory	Stone mason

4 (a) Why is it important for most secondary industries to be close to a motorway junction or a port?

   (b) Why is power supply no longer important for most secondary industries?

5 (a) Describe the data shown in Figure 3.29 (page 87). Remember to quote figures from the graph and describe the pattern you can see.

   (b) Explain at least three reasons for the pattern you have identified in part (a).

Extension questions

6 How can some of the environmental problems tourism creates for locals be overcome? Identify three environmental problems and as many solutions for each problem as you can.

7 The importance of location factors for secondary industry has changed over time since the Industrial Revolution and varies between types of secondary industry. Explain, using example industries, why this is the case.

8 'The present growth in tourism is sustainable due to developing countries developing tourism.' Discuss this statement using examples to illustrate your argument.

3.5 The Toyota car plant at Burnaston

Car manufacturing is one of the world's biggest secondary industries. It employs large labour forces in different countries throughout the world. During the 20th century car manufacturing was mainly located in the USA and Europe where companies such as General Motors, Ford and Volkswagen made and sold vehicles for their own markets. Today, like many other large industries, car manufacturing has experienced globalisation. Cars are being made by a wide range of companies, particularly those based in Asian countries such as Japan, for markets in hundreds of different countries. It is an incredibly competitive market so transnational companies such as Toyota need to plan carefully where to locate their factories.

Toyota is the fifth largest company in the world and the largest manufacturer of cars, with factories in 26 different countries worldwide (see Figure 3.34) making it a highly successful TNC. Much of Toyota's global success has been credited to its highly efficient management structure and assembly techniques, such as the 'just in time' method of production. Parts are delivered to the assembly line at the moment they are needed, which avoids storing parts, which can be expensive. The company crosses three sectors of the employment structure:

- Secondary workers **assemble** (put together) the pre-manufactured parts of the cars on an assembly line in Toyota's factories.

- Quaternary workers are employed to research, develop and design new cars.
- Tertiary workers sell Toyota cars at dealerships throughout the world.

Hybrid cars

In 1997 Toyota introduced its first hybrid car – the Toyota Prius (see Figure 3.35). These cars use a traditional petrol- or diesel-fuelled combustion engine to generate power but an electric battery is charged when using this power source, which can be used to power the car at other times (typically when cruising or at low speed). The electric battery is also charged when going downhill or decelerating. By May 2007, Toyota had sold one million hybrid cars worldwide.

■ **Figure 3.34:** Location of some of the major Toyota factories

■ **Figure 3.35:** The Toyota Prius

Toyota's reasons for moving car assembly to Britain

Toyota is a Japanese company and its headquarters and much of its car production remain in Japan. However, with an ever-increasing demand for its cars in Europe, Toyota decided to reduce transport costs and locate a car assembly plant in Europe to serve this market. The European market at this time was the largest in the world and Toyota was already selling 400 000 vehicles in Europe during the late 1980s.

Instead of locating the new car assembly plant in central Europe, Toyota decided that Britain would be the best country for its factory. This decision was made for several reasons:

- Britain had a history of car manufacturing, and therefore had labour with the appropriate skills to work in its factory.
- Despite being an island, Britain has excellent transport links to the rest of Europe.
- Britain has a large market for cars, therefore many cars that would be manufactured in Britain would also be sold in Britain.
- Car plants assemble parts, or components, at their factories. Britain already had many component manufacturers that could supply a Toyota factory with the parts it needed.

Toyota's reasons for choosing Burnaston

After deciding that Britain would be the host country for its factory, Toyota then had to decide where in Britain would be best and most profitable for the company.

After analysing several sites, Burnaston in Derbyshire (Figure 3.36) was chosen for the following reasons:

- Burnaston is centrally located in Britain and served well by the M6 and M1 motorways, so is an ideal location from which to transport the manufactured cars to markets in Britain and Europe (85 per cent of cars manufactured at Burnaston are exported to mainland Europe).

- There are many component factories located in the West Midlands which could supply a Toyota factory.
- Although centrally located in Britain the price of land in Derbyshire is relatively cheap, certainly compared to the prices of sites in the south of England.
- The large site at Burnaston was ideal because the land was flat and even after the factory had been built there would still be room for expansion (see Figure 3.37). This proved the right choice because Toyota did indeed expand in January 2001, increasing output from 100 000 to 170 000 cars per year.

■ **Figure 3.36:** Burnaston, Derbyshire

Similar location factors were considered when Toyota opened its Deeside factory in North Wales in 1992. In 2011, the Deeside factory employed 486 people, and the larger Burnaston factory employed 2662. However, due to the economic down turn that began in 2008, Toyota began to reduce working hours at its UK factories and in Japan closed its factories for eleven days to reduce output and stocks of unsold cars.

The Burnaston plant currently manufactures the Toyota Auris and Avensis models. In 2012 the plant produced 109 000 cars. A spokeswoman for the factory said: 'Our objective is to optimise the one production line that we have at Toyota

■ **Figure 3.37:** Toyota's factory at Burnaston

Manufacturing UK, which is capable of producing between 170 000 and 180 000 cars a year. At present, a car is rolling off our production line at a rate of one every 66 seconds.'

How Toyota benefits the local community

A committed workforce and innovative ideas have driven Japanese industry in recent years. These qualities are incorporated into the production processes employed by Toyota and are used in the UK factories. Toyota was well aware that to be successful at Burnaston it needed to gain the respect and support of the local community, by not only providing well-paid jobs but also offering excellent working conditions to its workers and consulting carefully with local government about the building of the plant.

After its expansion in 2001, Toyota employed around 2850 people. This helped to reduce unemployment in the local area and provided school leavers with a possible career. These workers are provided with very favourable working conditions which have helped to create a stable and happy workforce. These conditions include:

- Generous shift allowance
- Paid overtime
- 25 days' paid annual holiday (plus bank holidays)
- Private healthcare
- Pension
- Life assurance
- Attractive car plan
- Free workwear
- Subsidised restaurants
- Workplace nursery

Toyota's decision to locate its plant in the West Midlands has encouraged the development of further component manufacturers in the area which has been good for the local economy. Having seen Toyota's success at Burnaston other TNCs are now likely to choose Britain, and possibly the West Midlands, to locate their manufacturing plants.

3.6 Jaguar expansion at Solihull

Jaguar Land Rover is an example of a former British car manufacturing company which has been bought by a large foreign TNC, first Ford and now the Indian company Tata. Jaguar Land Rover has three plants in the UK, one of which is located in Solihull near Birmingham – less than 50 miles from Burnaston. Jaguar Land Rover chose this location for similar local and regional reasons to Toyota, and like Toyota is now looking to expand production as the global economy recovers from recession.

Jaguar Land Rover announced at the 2013 Geneva Motor Show that it would be creating 700 new jobs by investing an extra £165 million on expanding its engine manufacturing centre in Solihull. The near-100 000 sq m plant's expansion will bring the total number of jobs there up to 1400. Jaguar announced the site will be the home of a new breed of technologically advanced, lightweight, four-cylinder, low-emission diesel and petrol engines. The state-of-the-art facility is the first in the firm's history to be completely designed and specified by Jaguar Land Rover. The plant will include an engine testing centre alongside the manufacturing and assembly halls.

■ **Figure 3.38:** The production line at Jaguar in Solihull

Exercise 3E

1 Why did Toyota choose to locate its car factory in Britain? Use the terms below in your answer:

market	component manufacturers
skilled labour	transport

2 On a blank outline map of Britain locate Burnaston. Draw arrows pointing to Burnaston and write labels to show why this particular site was a good choice for Toyota.

3 Explain the meaning of each of the following words:

labour	Industrial Revolution
hi-tech goods	science parks

4 What benefits does Toyota bring to the community of Burnaston and the surrounding area?

5 Imagine that you are working for the recruitment department at Toyota's Burnaston car manufacturing plant. You want to attract the best workers to come to work in your plant. Create an advertisement to go in a national newspaper explaining the advantages of working for Toyota.

Extension questions

6 Explain what you think governments can do to attract TNCs such as Toyota to their countries.

7 **Jaguar is a successful British car manufacturer**. Is this statement true or a little misleading? If you have access to the internet this would be a good question to research.

3.7 Bangladesh factory collapse, April 2013

On 24th April 2013 an eight-storey building used for manufacturing clothing located on the outskirts of Bangladesh's capital city Dhaka collapsed, killing 1129 people and injuring 2500. Ranza Plaza contained clothing factories, a bank, apartments, and several other shops. The shops and the bank on the lower floors immediately closed after cracks were discovered in the building. However, warnings to avoid using the building after cracks appeared the day before had been ignored. Garment workers were ordered to return the following day and the building collapsed during the morning rush-hour.

■ **Figure 3.39:** Bangladesh, South East Asia

■ **Figure 3.40:** The collapse of Ranza Plaza, Dhaka

Why did Ranza Plaza collapse?

Unfortunately building collapse is a much more common occurrence in developing countries, such as Bangladesh, for several reasons:

- Cheaper and poorer quality building materials are used for construction. Buildings are often made nearly entirely from poor quality brittle cement without strong steel frameworks.
- There are fewer laws regulating (controlling) how buildings should be built in Bangladesh compared to Britain.
- Bangladesh cannot afford to employ as many people to check the safety of buildings after they have been built.
- The high population density in developing country cities such as Dhaka means most buildings have many storeys and are built very close to one another.

The Bangladeshi government blamed the owners and builders of the Ranza Plaza for using poor quality construction materials, including poor quality rods, bricks and cement, and not obtaining the necessary clearances. However, human disasters continue to happen in Bangladesh's factories. In November 2012, 114 people were killed in a factory fire, while a fire killed eight people at another garment factory in Dhaka just one month after the Ranza Plaza collapse.

Reshma's story

Emergency service workers pulled Reshma Begum, a seamstress who was working on the third floor of the factory, from piles of debris 17 days after its collapse. Reshma had been breathing through a pipe from inside the wreckage and, although trapped, had suffered no serious injury. Reshma told rescuers she had survived by scavenging for biscuits in the rucksacks of dead colleagues and drinking rainwater.

A woman crying near the wreckage said Reshma was her niece. 'We'd only expected to see her body,' she cried. As Reshma was lifted from the rubble, crowds at the site broke into cheers of

■ **Figure 3.41:** Reshma Begum is carried from the collapsed Rana Plaza building in Bangladesh

'God is great!' Rescue workers were seen wiping away tears. Army officers co-ordinating the rescue expressed astonishment at finding a survivor in the rubble. 'It is incredible that someone could have survived in the wreckage 408 hours after the building came down,' Lieutenant Shah Jamal said. 'Her will to live is amazing. We've given her oxygen and she has been rushed to hospital.'

What was the response of TNCs such as Primark?

The Ranza Plaza disaster threatened to damage the reputation of Primark and other TNC clothes manufacturers who use factories in developing countries, such as Bangladesh, to make their clothes.

Primark denies a link between the cheap clothes it sells in its shops in Europe and working conditions in developing countries. Primark's head of ethical trading, Katherine Kirk said after the disaster:

'We were doing as much if not more than other brands. We looked at all the risks we were aware of and were trying to reduce them and make sure people were working in safe places. We were not doing structural surveys and no other brand was doing structural surveys.'

Following the disaster, which involved manufacturers working for up to 40 companies, including British retailers Matalan and Bonmarché as well as Primark, more than 50 brands have signed up to a legally binding building safety agreement.

Many organisations are trying to halt the abuse of labour in developing countries. For example, the Clean Clothes Campaign is an international organisation whose aim is to end labour abuses in the clothes industry. The Campaign, for example, looks closely at operations in Asia (particularly Thailand), India and China and campaigns for better wages and fair working conditions in accordance with standards set by the International Labour Organization.

3.8 The effects of globalisation on industry

Why we should be concerned

As the 'consumers' of products made in developing countries and sold in clothes shops in our towns and cities, we have a moral responsibility to think about the welfare of those who have made the clothes we buy and wear. Of course it is all too easy to forget this when you are thinking about fashion and looking for a bargain.

Due to extreme poverty and a lack of education, people in developing countries are in desperate need of jobs. Therefore they are prepared to accept a low wage which may not give them enough to live on. Often they work very long hours in poor conditions. In developed countries, by contrast, unions would insist on a living wage and reasonable working conditions.

For example, a textile worker in a developing country may only be paid US$1.60 a day, but a meal may cost about 60–70 cents, which means the worker can only afford two meals per day. Therefore, there will be little remaining for accommodation. As many as ten people may sleep, eat and wash in a one room hut. Working conditions in the factories are often very unpleasant. Hundreds of people may be working long hours in a small space, with poor ventilation and limited access to drinking water. These labour intensive factories are therefore called sweatshops (see Figure 3.42 on page 97). Extreme poverty and lack of government regulation can mean that TNCs are able to exploit child labour.

Environmental damage and pollution may also occur as there are few laws in developing countries to ensure TNCs protect the environment.

Positive effects of globalisation

Globalisation does bring some benefits to developing countries.

When TNCs come into a country, they provide jobs which, together with goods being shipped out of the country (exports), should increase the country's wealth. Workers may gain skills, practical and managerial, that they may not otherwise have had the opportunity to gain. They and their children may also benefit from healthcare and/or education schemes provided by the TNC.

■ **Figure 3.42:** Sweatshop labour in South East Asia

Communities often benefit from an improved transport infrastructure, with new roads being built. Factories need energy so power supplies are improved. And, as one TNC moves in, others sometimes follow, thereby increasing the impact of these benefits.

The effect of globalisation on developed countries

As manufacturing jobs move to developing countries, manufacturing industries close down in developed countries and employees suffer job losses. However, the advantage of globalisation is that companies can often supply a greater range of cheaper products to their markets while maintaining and indeed growing their profits.

Geography in the news

TNCs change which countries they use for supplying their clothes regularly, so examples in textbooks of labour abuses in developing countries often become outdated. So why don't you do your own research and see what is happening out there in the real world right now? If you don't like what you find out you could even join an action group to help stop child labour or help to raise awareness of it.

Below is a list of useful websites which might be able to help you find out where in the world less wealthy people are working long hours, in poor conditions, for little pay, to make our clothes.

- www.sciencenewsforkids.org
- www.bbc.co.uk/newsround
- www.timeforkids.com
- www.firstnews.co.uk
- http://kids.nationalgeographic.com

Exercise 3F

1 (a) On a blank outline map of the world, label Bangladesh and its capital city Dhaka and shade in one colour.

   (b) Now label and/or shade the following location knowledge information (which you need to know for the CE examination):

   - India
   - China
   - Britain
   - Indian Ocean

   (c) Now write text bubbles which explain the reasons why factory disasters such as building collapses and fires are more likely in developing countries such as Bangladesh.

2 Imagine you were caught in the rubble of Ranza Plaza awaiting rescue, like Reshma Begum. Write 200 words to describe the conditions you face, what you would be feeling and why you might not want to work in a clothes factory if you survive your ordeal.

3 Explain the meaning of each of the following terms:

| sweatshops | labour intensive |
| regulations | living wage |

4 Investigate how and where any TNCs have exploited conditions in developing countries and write up you findings. You may need to do some research on the internet or in your library.

5 (a) Explain what actions Primark has taken to have a more positive effect in the developing countries where it has supplier factories.

   (b) What other efforts do you think TNCs could make to have more positive effects in the developing countries which supply their goods?

Extension question

6 Explain which different groups in society you think are responsible for preventing exploitation of low wages and unregulated working conditions in developing countries. Discuss measures those responsible could take to abolish these practices.

Exercise 3G: Enquiry suggestion

Whether you live in an urban or rural area there will be some forms of industry. Think about examples of primary, secondary, tertiary and quaternary industry in your local area and, with the help of your parents, contact one or more industries to ask them about what was important when they decided to locate their businesses where they have. Before you start you will need to design a questionnaire. Some of your questions should have 'closed answers' and some should allow for the industry employee you are interviewing to give more detail about location factors. When writing up your results, begin with a prediction, then explain the method of data collection you are going to use and locate the industry on a local map.

Exercise 3H

1 Solve the following clues:

(a) The process of spreading company ideas and business around the world (13 letters)

(b) A road built round a town (6 letters)

(c) Raw materials and goods transported by ship, train, lorry or other similar means of transport (7 letters)

(d) People who work in return for wages (6 letters)

(e) Chemicals sprayed on crops to kill insects and weeds that could damage the crop (10 letters)

(f) The sale of products to the public (6 letters)

(g) A line of transport, for example, road, rail, sea or air (8 letters)

(h) Pre-manufactured parts that are put together on an assembly line (10 letters)

(i) The process of an object being broken down naturally by nature (10 letters)

(j) Factories in developing countries that pack many workers into a small space, often with little ventilation or fresh water supply (10 letters)

2 Make a list of all the key terms in this chapter and their definitions. Check your definitions against the glossary on page 160.

4 Environmental issues

In this chapter, which underpins the topics of settlement, transport and industry, you will study:

- what constitutes the environment
- what environmental problems are being experienced on local, national and global scales
- the stewardship of environmental issues at different scales and how this is managed
- what specific environmental conflicts are occurring in the Peak District National Park and how these are being managed
- what specific environmental conflicts are occurring in the Tsavo National Park in Kenya and how these are being managed
- what is meant by sustainable development and how using renewable energy can aid sustainable development.

This chapter is particularly relevent to pupils studying towards the Common Academic Scholarship examination.

○ 4.1 What is the environment and why does it need protecting?

The environment and its future
The environment is the term used to describe three things:

- the landscape
- the <u>atmosphere</u> of a given area
- the wildlife, both plants and animals, which make it their home (habitat).

In the world today aspects of the environment (the landscape, the atmosphere and habitats) are being threatened and, in some cases, irreversibly damaged. Unfortunately these threats and subsequent damage are frequently due to the activities of human beings (see Figure 4.1). We are all responsible for preserving the environment and its resources for future generations. This concept is called **sustainable development**.

■ **Figure 4.1:** A river habitat damaged by human pollution

Sustainable development at different scales

Whether an environmental problem is small, such as litter in a park, or large and more difficult, such as global warming, it needs to be managed in order to promote sustainable development. Stewardship is the term that describes the role of those given responsibility for managing our environment at different levels.

Local scale

We can study and care for the environment on a local scale. Caring for the local environment involves assessing what threats exist to a village, town or city and its surrounding area. The local government is required to care for the local environment by providing services such as clearing up litter and recycling waste which reduces the amount of rubbish put in landfill sites. Local governments also enforce planning laws to prevent unrestricted building on greenfield sites, and creating preservation areas of countryside called Country Parks where wildlife can flourish. The local government is supported by many voluntary conservation groups which assist local schemes.

National scale

More widespread environmental problems on a national scale are the government's responsibility. The British government has a department called the Environment Agency which advises the government on the environment. It monitors pollution levels within our rivers and atmosphere, and can prosecute and fine offending companies. In the 1950s the government created National Parks (areas of natural beauty, such as Snowdonia in Wales) that it felt needed protecting from urban sprawl and activities that might damage the natural landscape and wildlife. Since then, the government has increased the number of National Parks in Britain to 15 and continues to preserve their landscape, wildlife and culture.

Many countries support the habitats, ecosystems and populations of certain animals that we term endangered. Although governments aid the protection of endangered species, charities such as the RSPB (Royal Society for the Protection of Birds) often take responsibility for this work.

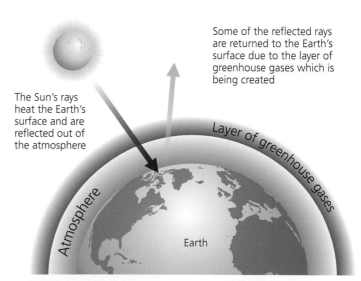

The Sun's rays heat the Earth's surface and are reflected out of the atmosphere

Some of the reflected rays are returned to the Earth's surface due to the layer of greenhouse gases which is being created

Atmosphere

Layer of greenhouse gases

Earth

■ **Figure 4.2**: The cause of global warming

Global scale

Some environmental issues need managing on a global scale:

- The most significant of these issues is global warming. Global warming can be defined as the artificial heating of our atmosphere, caused by the emission of gases such as carbon dioxide from cars, aeroplanes, industry, coal burning power stations and many other sources. These gases are referred to as greenhouse gases. As the concentration of greenhouse gases in the Earth's atmosphere increases, more of the energy radiated outwards from the surface of the Earth is held in the atmosphere rather than escaping to space, and the global temperature rises. This increase in global temperature is causing rapid change to many environments, impacting on biodiversity, including an increase in desertification, and the melting of the ice caps, leading to a rise in sea levels and possible flooding.

- Another environmental issue that needs addressing on a global scale is the preservation of environmentally unique regions such as Antarctica. Agreement between 46 different nations, including the USA, UK, China, South Africa and Australia, has seen Antarctica and its unique wildlife designated a global natural reserve under the *Protocol on Environmental Protection to the Antarctic Treaty*. This means Antarctica's land and sea resources are protected from destructive activities (see Figure 4.3).

■ **Figure 4.3**: Emperor penguins in Antarctica

Exercise 4A

1 Describe exactly what is meant by the term 'the environment'.

2 Write down whether each of the following is a *local*, *national* or *global* environmental issue:

> **global warming**
> **endangered species**
> **urban sprawl**
> **recycling**

3 (a) What is meant by the term 'conservation'?

　 (b) What parts of our environment need conserving and who takes responsibility for conserving each of these parts?

4 (a) Explain what is causing global warming. You may wish to draw a diagram to support your explanation.

　 (b) Who do you think is responsible for global warming? Explain your answer.

5 What is being done to conserve Antarctica's fragile environment?

Extension question

6 Education is the answer to developing a society that will protect the environment rather than abuse it. Discuss various methods of educating people about the environment on a *local*, *national* and *global scale*.

4.2 Sustainable development in the Peak District National Park

National Parks were developed in the USA as far back as the 19th century. In 1872 Yellowstone National Park was established as the world's first National Park. In a time of rapid settlement the US government decided that areas of natural beauty needed protecting. Then, as today, the US government owned most of the land within National Parks. In Britain the first National Parks were designated under the National Parks and Access to the Countryside Act 1949. British National Parks are different from those in many other countries, where they are owned and managed by the government. In England and Wales, land within a National Park is held largely in private ownership. This can lead to considerable conflict with the tourism industry.

The Environment Act 1995 defined the purpose of Britain's National Parks as:

1 Conserving and enhancing the natural beauty, wildlife and cultural heritage.
2 Promoting opportunities for the understanding and enjoyment of their special qualities.

The National Park Authority (NPA) must also support the economic and social wellbeing of local communities.

Attractions of the Peak District National Park

The Peak District National Park is one of Britain's most popular National Parks. Straddling the southern tip of the Pennines and covering much of Derbyshire, the Park has a varied landscape which includes limestone caves, wild moorland and rolling dales. Make sure you can locate the Peak District National Park on a blank map of Britain.

Visitors are attracted to the Park for a variety of reasons, but most come to enjoy the beautiful scenery and take part in outdoor activities such as hill walking, potholing and mountain biking.

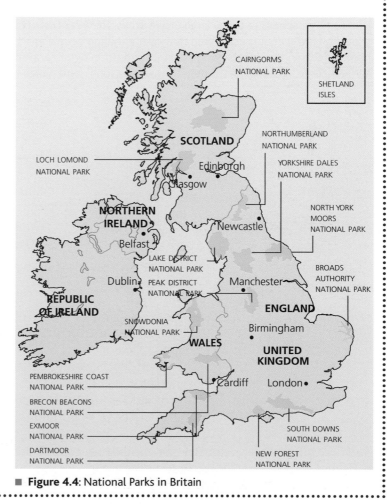

■ **Figure 4.4**: National Parks in Britain

The location of the Peak District makes it the most accessible National Park for many urban dwellers living in the Midlands and north-west of England. In fact, over 17 million people live within 95 km (60 miles) of the Park. It is the nearest large area of countryside to high population cities such as Manchester, Sheffield, Derby and Nottingham (see Figure 4.5). Easy road access, via the M1 and M6 motorways, results in the Park carrying up to 10 000 cars on its narrow roads each day. This figure increases significantly in the summer months and at weekends and bank holidays (peak periods). Additionally, unlike many other National Parks in Britain, the Peak District National Park is well served by public transport.

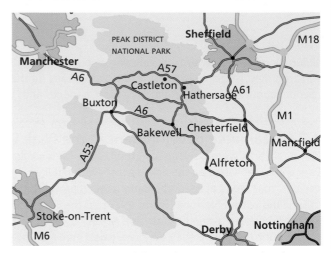

■ **Figure 4.5**: Location of the Peak District National Park

Benefits of tourism

Due to its closeness to many large urban areas, the Peak District National Park receives many day trippers. However, it is estimated that over a million people each year also stay overnight in the park at hotels, bed and breakfasts, youth hostels and camping or caravan sites. This provides many locals with some income, although often only through seasonal jobs, which may also be part time.

■ **Figure 4.6**: Landscape of the Peak District National Park

Locals may also be employed in shops selling outdoor equipment or souvenirs to tourists, or promoting conservation for the National Park Authority. In all, over £135 million is spent by tourists in the Peak District National Park each year, helping the National Park Authority to support communities such as Bakewell, a well-known honeypot site.

Conflicts of land use

Much of the Peak District National Park is privately owned by a number of organisations, such as the National Trust, trust estates and several water companies. There are around 2700 farmers in the Park in addition to forestry and limestone quarrying industries. Inevitably, conflicts occur between the different land users, local residents and tourist visitors. Here are two examples:

1 Conflict between tourists and local residents

There are often mixed feelings amongst local residents in National Parks about the influence of tourist visitors. Although tourist money often provides locals with jobs, there has been an increasing trend in recent years for wealthy outsiders to buy local houses for use as holiday homes. This reduces the already limited housing available for local people, and increases house prices to levels many locals cannot afford, forcing them to move away from the area.

2 Conflict between tourists and farmers

As the Peak District National Park is an upland area, the most common type of farming is pastoral farming. Only about half of the farms are enclosed (crops or cattle are fenced in) with sheep grazing freely in the remaining area. Tourists threaten this method of farming by trampling pastures by walking or mountain biking off the signed footpaths. Traditional dry stone walls – which are of cultural importance – are also damaged as people scramble over them. Gates are often left open, causing livestock to escape. Because the landscape does not necessarily look like a 'typical' farm, many tourists treat it as common land and believe they should be able to roam freely.

Environmental problems

Some landscapes and areas that are extremely beautiful and relatively easy to get to become particularly popular visitor attractions. They are often referred to as honeypot sites. These sites are encouraged because they concentrate the damage caused by tourists into a small area, thereby helping to make conservation easier in other parts of the Park. However, honeypots can suffer from overcrowding problems, littering, strain on facilities and transport networks, crime and erosion.

Although it is well served by public transport, 95 per cent of visitors to the Peak District National Park still arrive by car. This creates two problems:

- The narrow roads in honeypot locations can become highly congested, particularly at peak periods (see Figure 4.7).
- As a result of the heavy traffic, air pollution levels in the Park during June, July and August can be higher than similar recordings taken in central London.

■ **Figure 4.7**: Heavy traffic in Bakewell

Large numbers of walkers in a concentrated area can damage the landscape, and many of the 3000 footpaths in the park are now impassable. This leads to walkers leaving the footpaths and creating new paths, which damages the moorland vegetation that attracts tourists (see Figure 4.8). Footpath erosion is made worse by the use of four-wheel drive vehicles on tracks and mountain bikes on paths.

Litter is unattractive and can lead to fires on moorland. Broken glass, parts of tin cans and plastic bags can harm or trap wildlife,

■ **Figure 4.8**: Destruction of moorland

particularly birds, preventing them from feeding and causing starvation. Moorland is the natural habitat for many birds that nest on the ground and are therefore easily disturbed by tourist activity.

Damage to the environment can also take the form of noise pollution and disturbance of animals.

Solutions to promote sustainable development

It is the job of the Peak District NPA to find methods to create harmony between all the different users of the Peak District National Park, and to conserve the environment from damage caused by tourism. Some of the methods that have been used include:

- Educating visitors about the issues and encouraging responsible behaviour through the use of visitor centres and information boards.
- Creating stone pathways which are more resistant to erosion can reduce the risk of footpaths wearing away. Clear signs encourage most walkers to keep to the path provided and not stray onto sensitive moorland. Providing separate mountain biking and horse riding trails helps to prevent a conflict of use and further erosion.
- Encouraging a more responsible attitude to litter disposal and persuading visitors to take their rubbish home with them.
- Employing wardens or park rangers helps to encourage Park users to stick to the pathways and take care of the environment.
- To prevent a build up of air pollution, tourists arriving by car are encouraged to use car parks on the borders of the Park and take a bus to their destination ('park and ride'). Motorists choosing to drive into the Park face heavy parking fees, especially in the honeypot towns.
- Limiting the number of houses that can be sold to tourists keeps house prices down for local residents. Such a policy also prevents a decline in public services such as post offices, local shops and petrol stations which are supported by local residents on a regular basis rather than occasionally by owners of holiday homes.

Figure 4.9 summarises the problems and conflicts caused by groups in the Peak District National Park, the proposed solutions and the effects that these should have on people.

Conflict groups	Management problem	Solution	Effect on people
Tourists conflict with local residents in honeypot towns and villages by creating congestion and pollution with the additional cars.	Trying to prevent pollution and congestion with a method that will not stop visitors from coming to the Park.	Introduce park and ride schemes and charge high prices for use of local car parks.	Honeypot towns and villages have reduced congestion and pollution which will benefit locals and tourists alike. Local businesses such as shops, restaurants and hotels may not receive as much business.
Tourists conflicting with local farmers by leaving gates open and walking off footpaths, causing soil erosion.	Trying to protect the economic needs of farmers without undermining the sense of freedom that tourists come to the Park to enjoy.	Provide clearly marked signs and employ park wardens to enforce rules regarding closing gates and keeping to footpaths.	Local farmers feel that something is being done to protect their interests and will be more supportive of tourism. Tourists may feel that signposts and wardens prevent them roaming freely.
People from outside the local area conflict with locals by buying up properties in honeypot towns or villages to use as holiday homes.	Trying to ensure that local people can afford to buy property in the honeypot towns and villages and that local services are supported all year round. It is difficult to pass laws allowing only local residents to buy private properties.	Reserve a percentage of local housing for local people. Enforce a minimum occupancy period on holiday homes to ensure local services are supported.	Young people who are born in honeypot towns or villages have the opportunity to buy a house locally. Tourists are encouraged to engage with the local community if they buy holiday homes.

■ **Figure 4.9**: Solutions to conflicts in areas such as the Peak District National Park

Exercise 4B

1 What is the purpose of National Parks in Britain?

2 Why does the Peak District National Park attract so many visitors? Use the following terms in your answer:

   motorways
   urban areas
   honeypots

3 (a) What is meant by the term 'conflict'?

   (b) Choose two areas of conflict between different groups of people in the Peak District National Park and explain why conflict occurs.

4 What effect do you think wealthy tourists buying houses within National Parks may have on the residents of local communities? Consider particularly the effect on community services.

5 Propose solutions to limit the following impacts of tourism and industry that occur in the Peak District National Park:

(a) Noise and dust created from limestone quarrying.

(b) Damage to dry stone walls by walkers scrambling over them.

You will need to do some research to answer this question.

Extension question

6 Over 30 million people visit the Peak District National Park each year. Of these, 95 per cent arrive by car, causing large amounts of harmful air pollution. Does the NPA need to limit the number of visitors? Consider a possible solution to this problem and discuss the advantages and disadvantages of such a scheme.

Development and indicators of development

Most countries can be broadly placed in two groups:

● Wealthy countries such as Britain, the USA and many European countries are called More Economically Developed Countries.
● Poorer countries such as Ethiopia and Bangladesh are called Less Economically Developed Countries. Kenya is a developing country – a relatively poor country which is seeking to increase its wealth by encouraging tourists to visit and spend money.

There is a third group of countries called Newly Industrialised Countries or NICs, which are becoming wealthier due to the rapid growth of their manufacturing sector. China is an excellent example of a NIC. It cannot be classified as a developed country because only a very small percentage of its population enjoys the wealth and benefits of China's global dominance of manufacturing.

Poorer countries naturally try to increase their wealth in order to enjoy the benefits of a higher standard of living. Kenya and other developing countries such as Egypt, Thailand and India have tried to do this by encouraging the growth of tourism. They are hoping to follow the examples of countries such as Greece, Spain and Italy, which were relatively poor in the mid-20th century but are now prosperous developed countries, partly as a result of tourism. The wealth and standard of living of a country's population can be measured in a number of ways; these are called indicators of development:

● Gross Domestic Product (GDP) is defined as the total value of all goods and services produced within a country in one year.
● The total amount of money a country makes, plus the money it makes from foreign investments, is called the Gross National Product or GNP. GNP gives us an indication of how economically developed a country is, but it does not measure the standard of living experienced by a country's people.
● The Human Development Index (HDI) combines indicators of adult literacy rates, life expectancy and income to give a more balanced view of the level of development. Countries are given an HDI score between 0 and 1. A score nearer to 1 indicates a more developed country. For example, the HDI for the UK was 0.849 in 2010, whereas Niger's HDI was 0.261. Figure 4.10 shows how the HDI varies around the world.

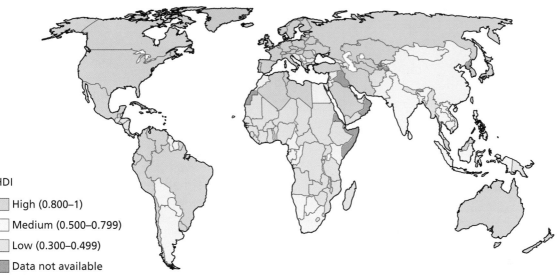

HDI
- ▨ High (0.800–1)
- ▢ Medium (0.500–0.799)
- ▨ Low (0.300–0.499)
- ▨ Data not available

■ **Figure 4.10**: World map showing the Human Development Index (HDI), 2010

4.3 Sustainable development in the Tsavo National Park, Kenya

Attractions of Kenya and the Tsavo National Park

Kenya has many physical advantages that make it very attractive to tourists. These are illustrated in Figure 4.12 (page 110):

- It has large areas of savannah grassland, the habitat for wildlife such as elephants, rhinos, buffalo, lions and leopards, the 'Big Five' that tourists come to see on safaris.
- The beautiful Great Rift Valley overlooked by Mount Kenya provides a challenging environment for walkers and mountain climbers (see Figure 4.11).
- Sandy beaches which line the Indian Ocean coastline attract tourists in search of relaxing holidays.
- Kenya's coastline has the added attraction of coral reefs which tourists may also choose to visit for scuba diving or snorkelling holidays.
- Tourists often prefer Kenya to other destinations as it offers many different activities as well as a pleasant climate.

■ **Figure 4.11**: Great Rift Valley landscape, Kenya

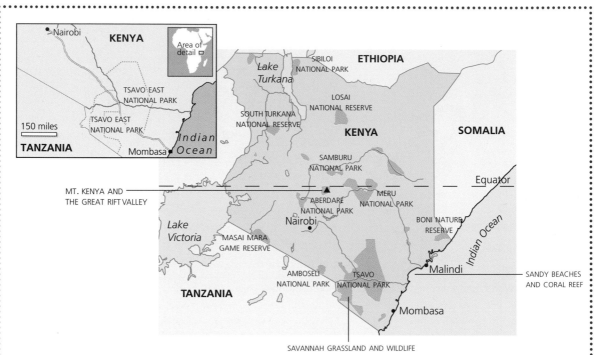

■ **Figure 4.12**: Map of Kenya highlighting its advantages for tourism

A distinct advantage for Kenya's economy is the fact that Kenya attracts tourists throughout the year. Figure 4.12 illustrates that Kenya is on the Equator, ensuring that it experiences sunny and consistently hot weather throughout the year. For this reason it is a particularly popular destination for European tourists in the winter months.

A principal tourist attraction in Kenya is the Tsavo National Park, a major wildlife reserve. The park covers an area bigger than Wales (21 812 sq km/8422 sq miles) and is split in two by the main road between Nairobi and Mombasa (Figure 4.12) to create Tsavo East and Tsavo West:

- Tsavo East is mostly flat semi-arid plains which support a variety of wildlife including the **'Big Five'** as well as less well-known species such as the blue monkey, the African civet and the white-tailed mongoose. In Tsavo East is the Mudanda Rock, a large permeable rock formation that attracts a lot of the region's rainfall and provides drinking grounds for the large elephant population.
- Tsavo West is more mountainous and wetter than Tsavo East and has a varied landscape that includes swamps, lakes and areas of savannah grassland which support the black rhino. Mizima Springs is a wetland area that has been adapted so that tourists can view hippos in their natural habitat through giant plate glass windows.

Although the Tsavo National Park is mainly renowned for its great elephant herds (see Figure 4.13), the network of roads and paths that cover over 800 km (500 miles) in the Park allows tourists to see a wide variety of animals, including reptiles such as the

■ **Figure 4.13**: Elephants in Tsavo East

crocodile and the black-necked cobra. The vegetation of the Park also provides the habitat for over 500 species of bird, including ostriches, herons, kestrels and kingfishers.

Benefits of tourism

The Kenyan authorities have permitted only one safari lodge within the Park itself in order to minimise the negative effects of tourism. However, several lodges have been built on the borders of the Park. These lodges provide employment for locals as guides for game viewing, walking safaris or bird watching. Because Tsavo is so close to the Indian Ocean, it attracts visitors from the coast. Therefore, many hotels have been built, which provide jobs for nearly 200 000 Kenyans. These are permanent, not seasonal, jobs. All hotels charge a tourist tax which the government puts towards developing Kenya's infrastructure (new schools, roads, hospitals and so on). Annually Kenya receives approximately 780 000 tourist visitors, generating over £300 million for the economy.

Conflicts of land use

The development of tourism to boost Kenya's economy has, however, created several conflicts of land use between local people and developers:

- Increased tourist numbers and additional safari vehicles crossing the dry soil, in order to get closer to the wildlife, have increased the level of soil erosion in the Tsavo National Park. Soil erosion damages vegetation and threatens the habitat supporting the wild animals that tourists have come to see.
- Many local communities that used to live along the Indian Ocean coast have been forced to leave their homes (forced migration) to make way for hotel developments.

Environmental problems

As well as the problems listed above, irresponsible tourists have further damaged the environment by touching and walking on coral reefs. Many people also consider the hotels built on the Indian Ocean coast to be visual pollution.

Social problems

The Kenyan government has a policy that one-quarter of income from tourist sites should benefit the local economy. However, difficulties at central and local government level have meant that this does not happen. Additionally, a large proportion of hotels in Kenya are in fact owned by multi-national corporations, such as Hilton or Hyatt-Regency, which are owned by American or European companies. Over 90 per cent of the profits leave the country, so money is rarely re-invested in the local infrastructure by such companies.

Although tourism creates permanent jobs in Tsavo National Park and other areas, the better-paid jobs such as hotel managers, childcare supervisors and water sports instructors are rarely awarded to local people.

Violent crime rates have soared in Kenya which is starting to have a significant impact on the number of tourists choosing it as a holiday destination.

Solutions to promote sustainable development

It is the job of the Kenyan government and Tsavo National Park Authority to find methods of creating harmony between the different land users in Tsavo National Park and to conserve the environment from damage caused by the impact of tourism.

To reduce the impact of soil erosion and other environmental threats from tourism, park wardens in Tsavo National Park enforce a strict code of conduct for visitors:

> **Code of conduct for visitors to Tsavo National Park**
> - It is forbidden to travel in an open vehicle while in the Park.
> - Stay in your vehicle all the time. Get out only at designated areas.
> - Off-road driving is not allowed. View the wildlife from a distance with binoculars.
> - Off-road driving destroys vegetation, might kill wildlife and could interfere with the daily routine of animals. The tracks formed become an eyesore.
> - Animals have a right of way. Do not harass them or make loud sounds – this might scare them and make them nervous. Patience pays!
> - Remember not to litter.
> - Remember: do not take anything but photographs and leave nothing but footprints.

To overcome the environmental problems caused by the rapid development of the Indian Ocean coast, the Kenyan government has now restricted development, and created a National Maritime Park along the coast north of Mombasa.

To deal with the number of multi-national chains of hotels and the fact that local people are rarely given the better paid jobs, the Kenyan government promotes Kenyan-owned hotels.

In order to reduce crime, the Kenyan government has invested some of the income generated from tourism in strengthening its police force, and has increased criminal penalties.

Figure 4.14 summarises the problems caused by conflict groups in the Tsavo National Park, the proposed solutions and the effects that these should have on people.

Areas of conflict	Management problem	Solution	Effect on people
Tourists in jeeps on safari cause soil erosion.	Trying to balance the need to prevent irreversible environment damage with the reliance of many locals on tourism. Encouraging tourism without exploiting or damaging the traditional way of life of tribespeople.	Limit size, frequency and routes of safari vehicles in order to reduce impact and prevent unneccessary soil erosion.	Tribes people living on the savannah have a better chance of maintaining their nomadic way of life. Local people running safaris may have a reduced income by limiting safari numbers.
Habitat destruction and deforestation caused by promoting hotel development.	As above. As above.	Strict limitations on lodge development in national parks. Tsavo has only one lodge, although several have been created on its borders.	The savannah, which is so important to the nomadic way of life of local tribespeople, is protected from development. Tourists may choose another country to take a safari due to limited accommodation options in Kenya's national parks.
Developers force locals off their land in order to make way for tourist accommodation.	Balancing tourism in a sustainable manner while trying to protect the traditional lifestyles of local communities.	Encourage developers to employ locals at their hotel developments. Protect land by creating national parks and marine reserves.	Local people have an income from a tourist industry job, e.g. a waiter. The cultural traditions of local people can be lost as they adopt a more westernised lifestyle.

■ **Figure 4.14**: Solutions to conflicts in Tsavo National Park

Exercise 4C

1 (a) Explain what is meant by the terms developed country and developing country.

   (b) Name five developed countries and five developing countries.

2 (a) Describe the geographical advantages that attract tourists to Kenya.

   (b) What is seasonal employment? Why are tourism jobs in Kenya not seasonal?

3 Imagine that you have just spent a day on safari in Tsavo National Park. Give an account of the landscape and wildlife you have experienced.

4 Draw a spider diagram with the words 'benefits of tourism for local people' written in the middle. Think of the advantages that tourism brings to the people of Kenya and add them as legs to your spider diagram. If you have time, illustrate each leg with a sketch.

5 (a) Describe one way in which tourism has damaged the environment in Kenya and provide possible solutions to overcome this damage.

   (b) Describe one way in which tourism has had a negative impact upon the people of Kenya and provide possible solutions to these negative impacts.

Extension question

6 In a report written by Mike Crawley (a freelance writer based in East Africa), the Dean of the Faculty of Forestry Resources and Wildlife Management at Moi University, Kenya, Professor Baraza Wangila, warns that 'Kenya's wildlife could become a victim of its own success at attracting tourists'. Discuss what you think is meant by this statement.

4.4 Sustainable development for the future

The concept of sustainable development

As we have seen, sustainable development is the idea of protecting our planet's environment and resources for future generations. Since the Industrial Revolution human beings have been extracting fossil fuels to supply our ever-growing demand for energy. This increase in demand has led to major environmental problems such as pollution, deforestation and global warming. Only relatively recently has the international community begun to address sustainable development to some degree at local, national and global levels. In 1992 world leaders met in Rio de Janeiro in Brazil for an Earth Summit and created two main policies to promote sustainable development: *The Rio Declaration on Environment and Development* and *Agenda 21.*

The Rio Declaration on Environment and Development set out 27 different principles to which the international community should adhere. For example, Principle 23 (Figure 4.15) was created to encourage member countries of the United Nations to protect the environment in countries where the local people were unable to practise sustainable development for themselves.

Agenda 21 set out methods in which sustainable development could be achieved at national and local levels but recognised that developing countries and poorer countries were at a disadvantage, and would need to be assisted in their efforts towards these methods.

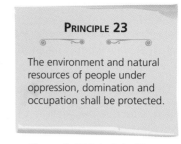

PRINCIPLE 23

The environment and natural resources of people under oppression, domination and occupation shall be protected.

■ **Figure 4.15**: Principle 23

Examples of sustainable development in developed countries and developing countries

Developed countries

Kirklees is a region in West Yorkshire with a high population density. It is sandwiched between Manchester to the west, Bradford and Leeds to the north and the Peak District National Park to the south (Figure 4.16). In response to the proposals of *Agenda 21* aimed at the local scale, Kirklees Metropolitan Council has come up with a plan for reducing transport problems and their impact upon the environment. Four travel-based targets have been identified by the council. Figure 4.17 shows each specific target, the aim of the target and the method by which the target may be achieved.

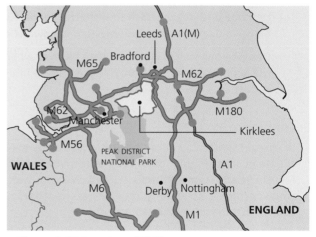

■ **Figure 4.16**: Location of Kirklees

Target	Aim	Method
1. To increase the number of people working from home.	To reduce the use of cars and resulting congestion/pollution, particularly at rush hour times.	Investing in information technology (IT) and promoting flexible working hours within local businesses.
2. To increase the number of residents working in Kirklees.	To prevent people using their cars to commute out of Kirklees.	Providing grants to encourage businesses to locate in Kirklees rather than elsewhere in the region.
3. To reduce congestion.	To reduce the pollution and related problems caused by congestion.	Possible schemes include building bypasses, charging high rates for town centre parking and allowing cars which have more than one occupant to use bus lanes or the hard shoulder of motorways (e.g. M62).
4. To increase the use of public transport.	To reduce congestion and pollution.	Invest in railways, bus services, and possible tram networks for larger settlements.

■ **Figure 4.17**: Kirklees Metropolitan Council travel-based targets

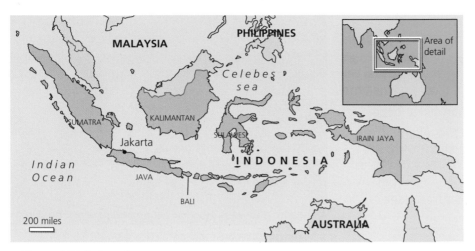

■ **Figure 4.18**: Indonesia

Developing countries

Look at the map of the islands that make up Indonesia (Figure 4.18) and in particular the islands of Java and Bali. Indonesia is a developing country with a population of over 200 million people and total land area of 1.9 million sq km (734 000 sq miles) resulting in a high population density. Around 44.3 per cent of the 95 million-strong workforce is employed in agriculture. As is the case in most developing countries, Indonesia is experiencing high population growth, resulting in more pressure on the land (such as deforestation) to meet the needs of the population.

The Indonesian island of Java practises **monoculture** of crops such as sugar, rubber (see Figure 4.19) and coffee which are grown for sale on the global market. These monocultures have grown as the global price of the commodities has reduced and Java's population has increased. This has led to serious soil erosion and nutrient depletion, as well as water pollution from pesticides.

However, the authorities in Java are studying the neighbouring Indonesian island of Bali (see Figure 4.20) as an example of how to practise agriculture in a sustainable way. Since the Rio Earth Summit of 1992, Bali has developed sustainable methods of farming, such as crop rotation which allows the soil to regain nutrients. In addition, farmers are encouraged to use alternatives to pesticides which limit environmental pollution.

■ **Figure 4.19**: A commercial rubber plantation in Indonesia

Renewable and non-renewable resources

Think about the demand you have made for energy today. From the moment you got up and switched on your bedroom light you have more than likely been using electricity to provide energy for all sorts of appliances. We can divide the resources that create energy into two simple groups: <u>renewable resources</u> and non-renewable resources (see Figure 4.21).

■ **Figure 4.20**: Women winnowing rice grains in a paddy field in Bali, Indonesia

Renewable resources	Non-renewable resources
● Will never run out	● Are produced by systems that are already in place
● Do not pollute the environment	● Are cheap to maintain
● Only work in specific locations	● Will run out in the future
● Can be destructive to the environment	● Pollute the environment
● Are expensive to concentrate	
Include	**Include**
● Solar	● Coal
● Geothermal	● Oil
● Hydroelectric power (HEP)	● Natural gas
● Wind	● Nuclear
● Tidal	

■ **Figure 4.21**: Renewable and non-renewable resources

Non-renewable resources include the raw materials of three main fossil fuels (oil, coal and natural gas) as well as nuclear power. They are non-renewable because they are sources of power that have taken millions of years to form and cannot be replaced once they are used. It has been predicted that all fossil fuels will run out within the next 200 years assuming nothing is done to find new reserves or develop any new processing technologies. Fossil fuels pollute the environment when burnt in power stations or used in car engines. As we have already learnt, global warming and its associated problems have been caused by a greater concentration of greenhouse gases in the Earth's atmosphere.

Nuclear energy is produced by splitting or fusing the nuclei of atoms; uranium is a material frequently used in this process. The advantages of nuclear energy are that a small amount of raw material produces a large amount of energy and doesn't give off atmospheric pollutants. The raw materials are relatively cheap. The disadvantages are that the radioactive waste from nuclear power plants has to be encased in iron and concrete and buried below the ocean surface to minimise damage to the environment. Accidental leakage of nuclear materials can have a devasting impact.

Alternative energy is made from renewable resources such as HEP, solar and wind power will never run out. However, they tend to be expensive to install and maintain and it is costly to concentrate the energy extracted. They are usually landscape/location specific:

■ **Figure 4.22**: Wind farm in Cornwall

● <u>Geothermal energy</u> can only be made use of in tectonically active areas such as Iceland or New Zealand.
● Wind turbines need to be located in areas that receive a continuous <u>prevailing wind</u> such as the west coast of Britain (see Figure 4.22).
● HEP dams must be in highland areas to create a suitable dam wall and reservoir.

Destruction of the environment can also be caused when valleys are flooded and tidal barriers and wind farms are erected. However, many renewable resource technologies are still being researched although they may never provide sufficient energy on a national or global scale.

Since the Industrial Revolution, developed countries have relied on fossil fuels to power industry and supply their demands for energy. More recently nuclear power has also provided a significant amount of energy in developed countries along with an increasing input from renewable resources, particularly HEP. In France, for example, nuclear power stations now account for 78 per cent of energy production (according to the EIA International Energy Annual 2005). Because

■ **Figure 4.23**: Dinorwig HEP station in North Wales

117

developing countries are limited by both their landscape/location and their wealth, these countries typically still rely on fossil fuels.

Dinorwig HEP station in North Wales

One of the British government's earliest attempts to provide a sustainable regional energy resource by harnessing water power was the construction of the HEP station at Dinorwig in North Wales (see Figure 4.23). The power station was built into the mountainside on the edge of Llyn (lake) Peris in 1984. A reservoir was created further up the mountain (see Figure 4.24) from which water flows with great force down

■ **Figure 4.24**: Upper reservoir at Dinorwig, North Wales

the slope, powering the six large turbines. During off-peak electricity periods (when demand for electricity is much lower) the water is then pumped back up to the higher reservoir. Other HEP stations are built near fast-flowing rivers in highland areas (see Figure 4.25).

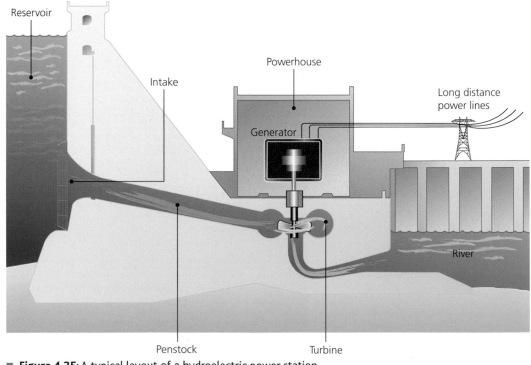

■ **Figure 4.25**: A typical layout of a hydroelectric power station

A high dam wall is built to bridge the valley and the area behind the dam wall will then be flooded to create a reservoir. This can be used to supply fresh water to the local and neighbouring regions, as well as being used for tourist and leisure activities such as fishing, waterskiing and sailing. Building dams and reservoirs on upland rivers also allows the authorities to control the flow of water into the flood plain, thereby reducing the possibility of flooding in winter months.

The disadvantage of such HEP schemes is the cost, not only of building and maintaining the dam wall, but also of buying the land that will form the reservoir. In addition, there may be environmental impact on river wildlife.

Exercise 4D

1 (a) What is sustainable development?

(b) What can be done on a local scale to aid sustainable development? Refer to examples in your local community if you can.

2 Draw a spider diagram to show how Kirklees Metropolitan Council has responded to the proposal of *Agenda 21*.

3 Create a flow chart to illustrate the demands for energy that you make in a typical day.

4 (a) Write sentences to define the following terms:

renewable resources
non-renewable resources
fossil fuels

(b) Why is it a good idea to replace non-renewable energy resources with renewable resources?

5 How can energy be generated from water? Refer to the Dinorwig power station example. You may wish to draw a diagram to help your explanation.

Extension question

6 Referring to examples in developed countries and developing countries, explain why sustainable development needs to be adopted on local, national and global scales.

Exercise 4E: Enquiry suggestion

The environment is a good topic to debate. Choose a chairman and speakers to debate any of the following motions:

- All visitors to National Parks should be charged for entry with or without a car.

- The government has no right to penalise individuals for having vehicles that produce a lot of carbon dioxide.
- The land from which locals have been evicted to make way for tourism in Kenya should be returned to them immediately.

Exercise 4F

1 Solve the following clues.

(a) Managing and caring for a place or area by a charity, private body or government (11 letters)

(b) Collecting waste materials and making use of them again (9 letters)

(c) The disposal of waste in natural or man-made holes in the ground (8 letters)

(d) The natural and human features of an area (9 letters)

(e) The number and variety of all living things within an ecosystem (12 letters)

(f) Contamination of the environment by gases, noise, litter or waste produced by individuals or industry (9 letters)

(g) The mass of gases surrounding the earth (10 letters)

(h) How rich or poor a country is in comparison with other countries; measured by indicators such as GNP, health standards, life expectancy, and so on (11 letters)

(i) An area displaying a distinctive interaction between plants, animals and the physical environment (9 letters)

(j) The cutting down and clearing of forested areas, which often leads to soil erosion and other environmental consequences (13 letters)

2 Make a list of all the key terms in this chapter and their definitions. Check your definitions against the glossary on page 160.

5 Location knowledge

■ **Figure 5.1:** A satellite image of the world

Location knowledge is your knowledge of where places are in the world. At the beginning of the Common Entrance examination there is a specific 'location knowledge' section which is worth approximately 15 marks. It is useful therefore to learn all the information in this chapter well, so you do not waste time pondering where to plot a capital city or trying to think of the name of a river.

Geography for Common Entrance: Physical Geography provides the location knowledge information you need to know by the end of year 6. This chapter includes all the information in *Physical Geography* and adds the final extra layer of information you need to have covered by the end of year 8 to be successful in this area of the Common Entrance examination.

In this chapter you will study:

● the location of the world's major physical features, such as continents and mountain ranges
● the location of the imaginary lines plotted on the globe such as the Equator and the tropics of Cancer and Capricorn
● the location of the physical features of Britain that you need to know for the exam
● the name, location and capital city of countries in each continent
● the location of other major cities across the globe
● how to revise location knowledge information for the exam.

◯ 5.1 The world's major physical features

What you need to know

Location knowledge requires you to be able to name and place many of the world's well known physical features. Such features include the world's continents, oceans and important rivers and mountain ranges. You will find a detailed list of exactly what you need to know below. Figures 5.2 and 5.3 on page 124 and Figure 5.4 on page 125, illustrate this information on a world base map. It is very easy to think you know this basic information about the world's physical features but make sure you can locate accurately all the physical features listed below, otherwise you may lose easy marks in this part of the exam.

Continents:	Africa, Antarctica, Asia, Oceania, Europe, North and South America
Oceans:	Arctic, Indian, North and South Atlantic, Pacific, Southern
Mountain ranges:	Alps, Andes, Himalayas, Pyrenees, Rocky Mountains
Deserts:	Sahara
Rivers:	Amazon, Mississippi, Nile, Rhine, Ganges, Yangtze

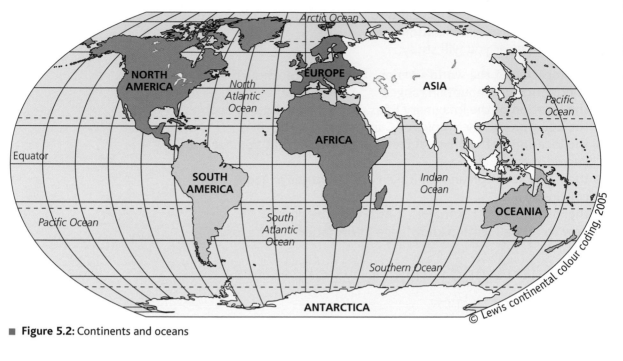

■ **Figure 5.2:** Continents and oceans

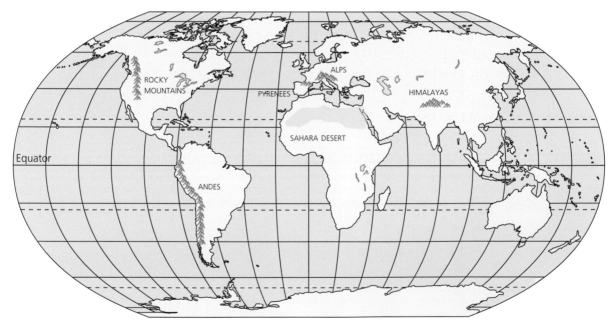

■ **Figure 5.3:** Mountain ranges and deserts

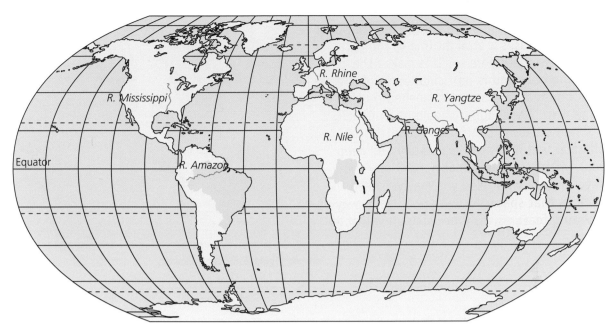

■ **Figure 5.4:** Rivers

How an exam will test your knowledge

Most questions testing location knowledge in an exam require short answers and are based on an atlas-style map of Britain, the world or any of the continents.

There are basically two methods that could be employed in an exam to test that you know where the world's major physical features are located.

● There may be letters on the map you are provided with and you will be expected to name, for example, the mountain range marked A or the river marked B.
● You may be asked to plot the location of, for example, the Sahara Desert.

When plotting information on a map be sure to be accurate and clear, to avoid losing marks. Use a sharp pencil, so that if you make a mistake you can correct it. If you are shading an area to represent a desert or mountain range remember that the area you cover needs to be accurate, particularly when it comes to crossing international borders. Look at Figures 5.5 and 5.6. They show a good way and a bad way of answering the question 'shade and label the Alps mountain range on the map of Europe'. Notice the differences between the strong and weak answer. The

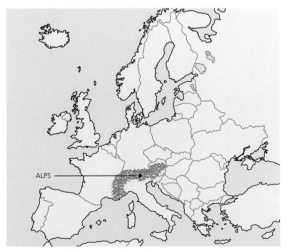

■ **Figure 5.5:** Strong answer

strong answer is spelt correctly, shades the correct area, crossing the correct international borders and uses a straight line to indicate where the label refers to. This makes the labelling neat and is particularly useful if more than one feature has to be labelled on the same map. The shading should be in pencil.

When labelling continents, countries or physical features, spell accurately and keep your writing to a reasonably small size; you have no idea what else you may yet need to label in that space. Arrows are a useful way of labelling features without using up valuable space.

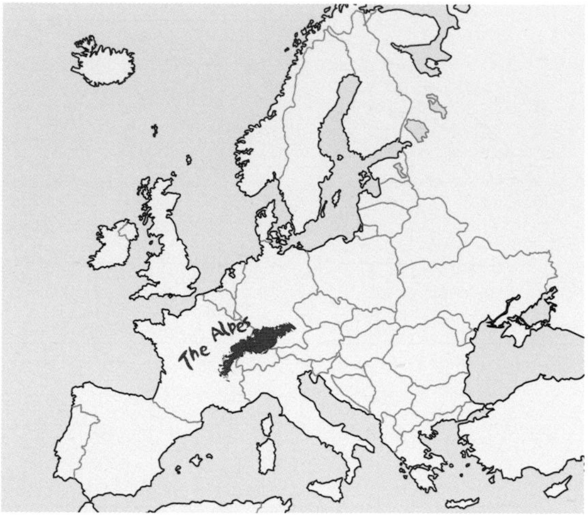

■ **Figure 5.6:** Weak answer

➡ Exam tip

Use Figure 5.2 to Figure 5.4 (pages 124–125) or an atlas to check that you know the exact location of all the major world physical features you are required to know for your exam. Use blank maps of Britain, Europe and the world to plot all the physical features. Blank maps are available for download from the Galore Park website www.galorepark.co.uk

Repeat this process several times before your exam so you know the information by heart. You could colour the maps and put them on your bedroom walls as a revision aid.

Exercise 5A

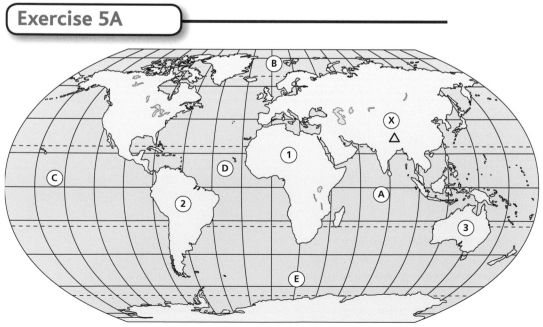

■ **Figure 5.7:** Test map

1 Name the seven continents.

2 Look at the map in Figure 5.7. Match each of the letters A to E with the name of an ocean.

3 Look at the map in Figure 5.7. Which number represents the Sahara Desert?

Extension questions

4 List the mountain ranges you need to know and which continents they are in.

5 List the rivers you need to know and name the seas or oceans they flow into.

6 The △ represents the world's tallest mountain, Everest, in mountain range **X**. What is the name of mountain range **X**?

5.2 The British Isles

What you need to know

From time to time the location knowledge aspect of an exam will be based on a map of Britain and will test your knowledge of the different physical features of the British Isles such as important rivers, mountain ranges and sea areas. However, you also need to know about human features such as the location of national borders as well as major cities and towns. You will find a detailed list of exactly what you need to know on page 128. Figures 5.8 and 5.9 illustrate this information on British Isles base maps. It is very easy to think you know this basic information about Britain's features but make sure you can locate accurately all the features shown below otherwise you may lose easy marks in this part of an exam.

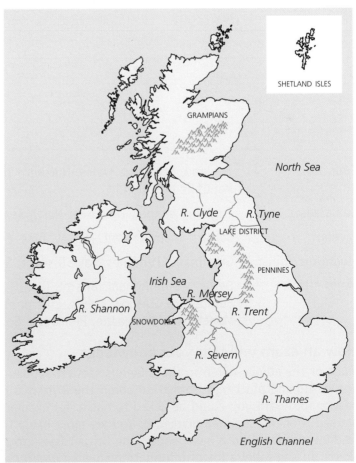

■ **Figure 5.8:** The British Isles: physical features

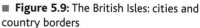

■ **Figure 5.9:** The British Isles: cities and country borders

Countries:	England, Scotland, Wales, Northern Ireland, Republic of Ireland
Sea areas:	English Channel, Irish Sea, North Sea
Rivers:	Severn, Thames, Trent, Mersey, Tyne, Clyde, Shannon
Mountains/hills:	Grampians, Pennines, Lake District, Snowdonia
Major cities:	Belfast, Birmingham, Bristol, Cardiff, Dublin, Edinburgh, Glasgow, Leeds, Liverpool, London, Manchester, Newcastle, Plymouth, Southampton

How an exam will test your knowledge

Much of the advice given in the previous section applies when answering and plotting information about the British Isles on a blank base map. Again you could be asked to name, for example, the river marked A or the sea area marked B. You are more likely to be asked to draw and label on a base map of the British Isles. You may need to sketch in and label a lot of information so even greater accuracy and neatness is necessary.

It is important to remember that the British Isles is essentially comprised of two sets of isles: the United Kingdom and the Republic of Ireland. Great Britain is the name given to the three nations of England, Wales and Scotland. Together with Northern Ireland, this comprises the United Kingdom. It is useful to know where the borders are between these nations and be able to draw them onto a base map of the British Isles.

> ### → Exam tip
>
> Use Figures 5.8 and 5.9 (pages 127–128) or an atlas to check that you know the exact location of all the major physical features of the British Isles you are required to know for your exam. Don't forget you also need to know the location of human features such as the major cities. Use blank maps of Britain to plot all the physical features and human features. Repeat this process several times before your exam so you know the information by heart. You could colour the maps and put them on your bedroom walls as a revision aid.

Exercise 5B

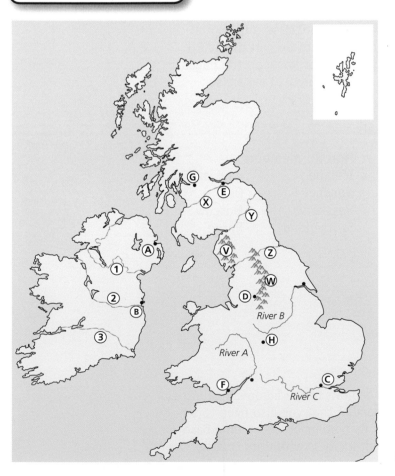

■ **Figure 5.10:** Test map

Referring to the Figure 5.10 above:

1 Name the three rivers marked A, B and C.

2 Name the port cities that are marked A, B and C on the map.

3 Which is the correct border between England and Scotland: line X, Y or Z?

Extension questions

Again refer to Figure 5.10 above:

4 Name the cities marked D, E, F, G and H.

5 (a) Which is the correct national border of Northern Ireland: 1, 2 or 3?

   (b) Which country does Northern Ireland border?

6 Name the mountainous area marked V and the mountain range marked W.

5.3 Countries, capitals and major cities

What you need to know

There are 28 European Union countries. Fortunately you only need to learn the location and capital city of 12 of these countries for the Common Entrance examination, as well as the location and capital city of 4 European countries which have opted not to be part of the EU.

You will find lists of exactly what you need to know on the pages that follow. Figures 5.11, 5.12 and 5.13 on pages 131–133 also illustrate this information.

European countries and their capitals

EU members		Non EU members	
Belgium	Brussels	Iceland	Reykjavik
Denmark	Copenhagen	Norway	Oslo
France	Paris	Russia	Moscow
Germany	Berlin	Switzerland	Berne
Greece	Athens		
Italy	Rome		
Netherlands	Amsterdam		
Poland	Warsaw		
Portugal	Lisbon		
Spain	Madrid		
Republic of Ireland	Dublin		
United Kingdom	London		

It can be straightforward to learn the capitals of the European countries within the syllabus, but you must remember that you also need to be able to recognise each country should its borders be drawn on a base map and be able to plot where the capital city is within its country.

■ **Figure 5.11:** European countries and their capitals

World countries and their capitals

You need to be able to identify the following world countries and be able to plot them on a world map, and know their capital cities (see Figure 5.12).

North America

Canada   Ottawa
Mexico   Mexico City
USA   Washington DC

South America

Brazil   Brasilia
Argentina   Buenos Aires
Chile   Santiago
Columbia   Bogota
Peru   Lima

Africa

Egypt   Cairo
Ethiopia   Addis Ababa
Ghana   Accra
Kenya   Nairobi
Nigeria   Abuja
South Africa   Pretoria

Asia

Afghanistan	Kabul
Bangladesh	Dhaka
China	Beijing
India	New Delhi
Indonesia	Jakarta
Iran	Tehran
Iraq	Baghdad
Japan	Tokyo
Pakistan	Islamabad
Russia	Moscow
Saudi Arabia	Riyadh
South Korea	Seoul
Thailand	Bangkok

Oceania

Australia	Canberra
New Zealand	Wellington
Papua New Guinea	Port Moresby

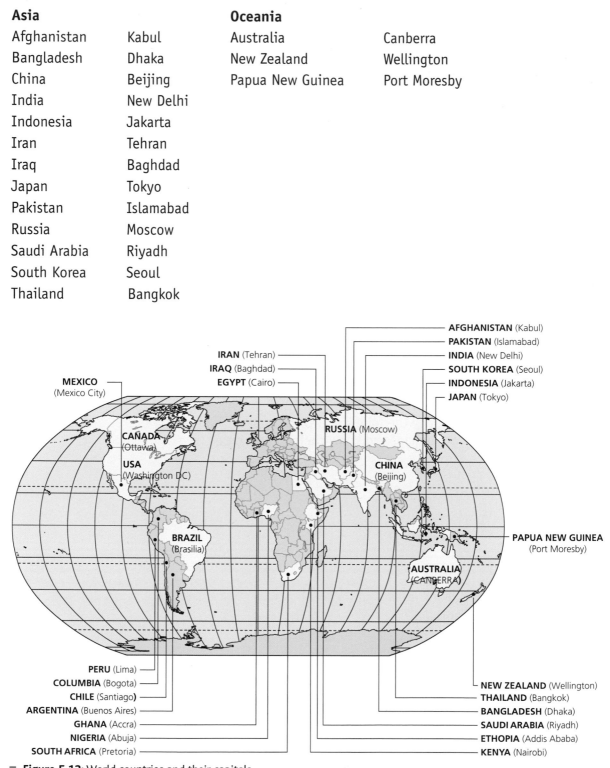

■ **Figure 5.12:** World countries and their capitals

Major cities

You will also need to be able to plot on any given base map the exact location of the following major cities. These are important cities but are not necessarily the capitals of their countries. You will find these cities plotted on Figure 5.13 and listed below:

Dubai	(UAE)
Kolkata	(India)
Los Angeles	(USA)
New York	(USA)
Rio de Janeiro	(Brazil)
Sao Paulo	(Brazil)
Shanghai	(China)
Sydney	(Australia)
Vancouver	(Canada)

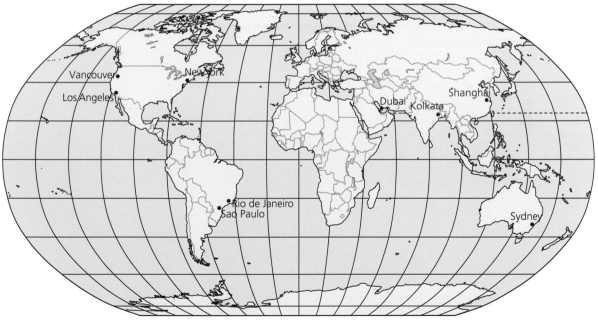

■ **Figure 5.13:** Major cities

How an exam will test your knowledge

Most commonly you will be asked to identify countries or cities marked by letters on a base map of either Europe or the world. If you are asked to shade and label a country on a base map, make sure you draw the borders of the country accurately, shade the country neatly and label it carefully. If you are asked to plot a city on a map, be sure to plot it accurately and spell it correctly.

Exercise 5C

1 Look at Figure 5.14 on page 135. Name the countries marked A, B, C, D and E.

2 Look at Figure 5.14 on page 135. Name the capital city of countries A, B, C, D and E.

3 Look at Figure 5.15 on page 135. Which of the countries marked X, Y and Z is Kenya?

4 Look at Figure 5.14.

   (a) Name the country marked F.

   (b) Name the capital city of the country marked F.

   (c) Is the capital city located at point 1 or 2 with country F?

5 Look at Figure 5.15 on page 135. If you travelled in a straight line from the countries labelled as 3 and 4 you would cross five countries. Name these countries.

6 Look at Figure 5.15.

   (a) Name the country marked 1 on the world map.

   (b) Name the country marked 2 on the world map.

   (c) Name the two countries that border country 2.

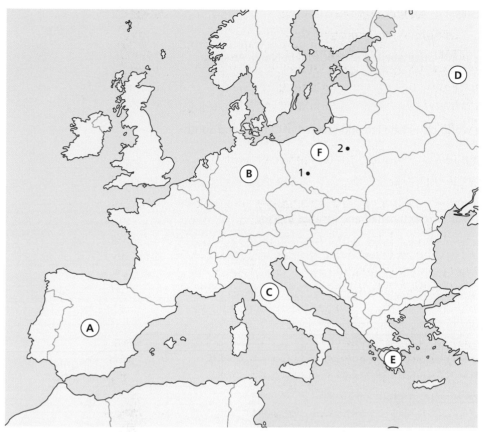

■ **Figure 5.14:** Countries and capitals European test map

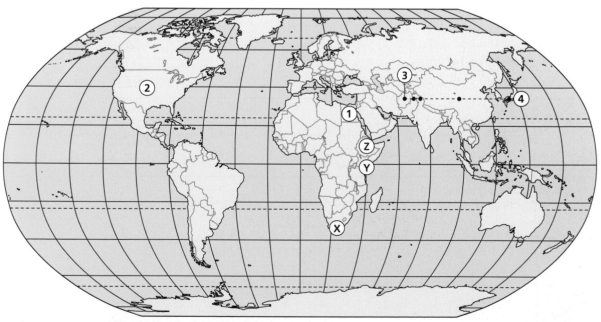

■ **Figure 5.15:** Countries and capitals world test map

Extension questions

Look at Figure 5.16.

7 Name the following world cities labelled and located in North America.

    (a) 1

    (b) 2

8 Name the following world cities labelled and located in Central and South America.

    (a) 3

    (b) 4

9 Name the following world cities labelled and located in Asia.

    (a) 5

    (b) 6

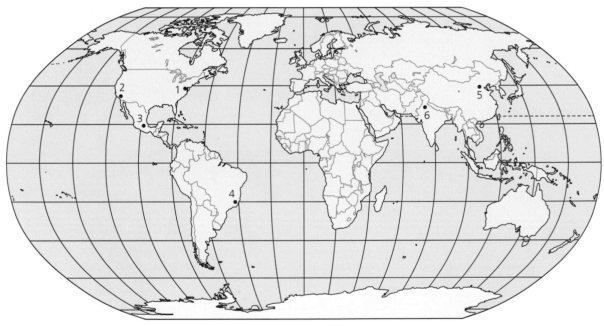

■ **Figure 5.16:** Cites world test map

5.4 Other features of the globe

What you need to know

There are several other pieces of information that you need to know for the location knowledge section of a syllabus. The information you need to know is shown on the world map in Figure 5.17.

You must be able to recognise, and possibly plot on a world base map, five different lines of latitude. Lines of latitude are the imaginary lines that run around the globe horizontally. The Equator is the line of latitude that runs round the centre of the globe and is given a value of 0°. From the Equator the North Pole is at a 90 degree angle or bearing, so we say the North Pole is 90° north. The South Pole is also at a 90 degree bearing from the Equator, so we say the South Pole is 90° south. You need to be able to plot the location of the North and South Poles.

In between the Equator and the poles are four other lines of latitude. These are the Tropic of Cancer at 23.5° north, the Arctic Circle at 66.6° north, the Tropic of Capricorn at 23.5° south and the Antarctic Circle at 66.6° south.

The imaginary lines that run around the globe vertically are called lines of longitude. You must be able to identify on a world base map only two different lines of longitude. Firstly, the Prime Meridian (also called the Greenwich Meridian) which is given a value of 0° and which runs from the North Pole to the South Pole through London. Secondly,

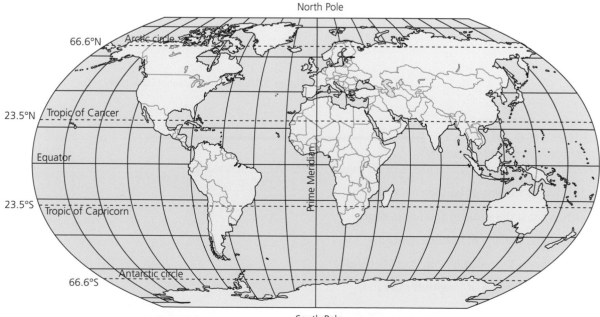

Figure 5.17: Other features of the globe

the International Date Line which runs from the North Pole to the South Pole on the other side of the globe to the Prime Meridian and has a value of 180° (see Figure 5.18).

Lines of longitude combined with national borders determine the time zones of the world. The sun rises to the east of the International Date Line and sets to the west of it. This means that as you travel east of Britain you have to put your watch forwards. If you travel to the west of Britain you have to put your watch backwards.

How an exam will test your knowledge

You will not be asked to draw lines of latitude or longitude onto a base map but you are likely to be asked to identify unlabelled lines such as the Equator or the International Date Line. Be sure to label these lines in clear but small letters on a base map as you may need to add further information in questions that follow.

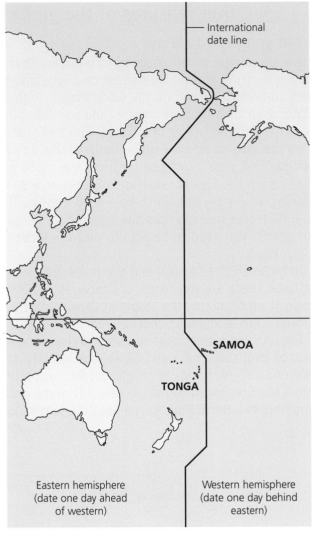

■ **Figure 5.18:** The International Date Line

Exercise 5D

Referring to the world map (Figure 5.19 on page 139) answer the following:

1 (a) Name the line of latitude marked A.

   (b) What is the value of this line in degrees?

2 (a) Name the line of latitude marked B.

   (b) What is the value of this line in degrees?

3 (a) Name the line of longitude marked C.

   (b) What is the value of this line in degrees?

5 Location knowledge

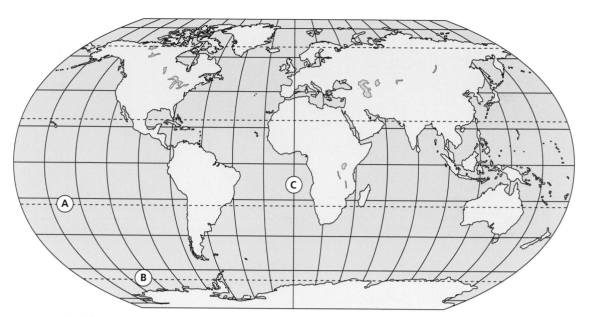

■ **Figure 5.19:** Other features of the globe and other world cities test map

Exercise 5E: Enquiry suggestion

To help learn all the information for the location knowledge section of the exam why not make it interesting by creating a game? There are many different quiz shows; you could choose the same format as one of the popular quiz shows and create questions based on the information you have to learn. If you and your friends created different types of quiz you could try them out on each other, maybe with the help of your Geography teacher, and improve your location knowledge and have fun while you are doing it!

Exercise 5F: Past exam questions

The following questions are taken from recent past papers. You will be asked to label features on a world base map which you can download from the Galore Park website www.galorepark.co.uk.

Look at the world map (Figure 5.20 on page 140).

1 Name the countries marked A, B and C on the world map. (3 marks)

2 Name the mountain ranges marked X, Y and Z on the world map. (3 marks)

3 On a world map, mark and name the following cities:

(a) Beijing (1 mark)

(b) Washington DC (1 mark)

(c) Madrid (1 mark)

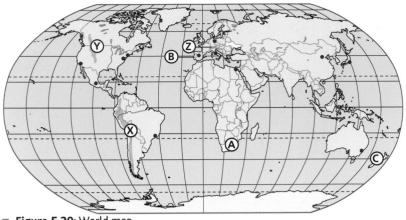

■ **Figure 5.20:** World map

4 If you fly east from Canada to France,

   (a) which ocean will you cross? (1 mark)

   (b) will you put your watch forward or back? (1 mark)

5 **(a)** What is the name of the tropic which passes through Egypt? (1 mark)

   (b) What is the capital of Egypt? (1 mark)

   (c) What is the name of the river which flows through Egypt? (1 mark)

Exercise 5G: Location knowledge summary crossword

Solve the following clues:

1   Capital city of Poland (6 letters)

2   Irish river (7 letters)

3   South American mountain range (5 letters)

4   Mountainous area in north of Wales (9 letters)

5   Country to the east of China (5 letters)

6   Capital city of Afghanistan (5 letters)

7   African river which flows through Egypt (4 letters)

8   Capital city of India: New . . . . (5 letters)

9   City in the north west of England (10 letters)

10 American river that flows into the Gulf of Mexico (11 letters)

6 Essential exam technique

■ **Figure 6.1:** Taking an exam

Many pupils are disappointed by their performance in exams. This is often because they have revised the Geography topics well but have been let down by poor exam technique. This chapter will help you with this essential aspect of doing well in the Geography exam by:

- explaining how the Geography paper is structured and what type of questions will be posed.
- showing you where the majority of marks are available and for what skills or knowledge they are awarded.
- Showing what command words could be used in questions and how to respond to them.
- Advising you on what mistakes are often made in the exam and how to avoid them.
- Illustrating examples of strong and weak answers.

◯ 6.1 The Common Entrance Examination

The structure of the exam

In 2013 a new Geography Common Entrance syllabus was published with many content changes. However, the style and layout of the CE paper remains similar to the papers used for examinations under the previous syllabus. The focus remains on a need for pupils to be able to apply skills they have developed throughout the course. Although there is no specific case study section in the CE paper detailed examples will be required in section C of the examination, where the following topics will be tested: earthquakes and volcanoes; weather and climate; rivers and coasts; population and settlements; transport and industry.

The exam is in three parts: Section A (approximately 15 marks), Section B (approximately 15 marks) and Section C (approximately 50 marks). The fieldwork project is worth 20 marks. The information below shows the areas covered in each part of the exam and the Geography for Common Entrance textbook in which each subject is covered.

Section A: Location knowledge (approximately 15 marks)

Location knowledge   Physical and Human Geography

Section B: OS mapwork (approximately 15 marks)

OS mapwork   Physical and Human Geography

Section C: Thematic studies (approximately 50 marks)

1. Earthquakes and volcanoes   Physical Geography
2. Weather and climate   Physical Geography
3. Rivers and Coasts   Physical Geography
4. Transport and Industry   Human Geography
5. Population and Settlement   Human Geography

Shorter answer questions

Question focus and format

Most questions in the exam require you to write a couple of lines to explain and answer. This style of question demands knowledge and skills from a wide variety of topics that you will have studied in class and more skills based on data response type questions. There are typically around five separate questions, each with several parts, in section C of the exam. Questions are layered in that they may offer one or two opening questions where only a few marks are awarded for identifying a physical feature or demonstrating a map skill (see Figure 6.2).

6 Essential exam technique

(142)

Remember that the Ordnance Survey map that comes with the exam paper will be at either a 1:25 000 or 1:50 000 scale. There will be a scale ratio on the bottom of the map and a full key to tell you what all the map symbols mean. Although a key is provided, it will save you time to know the common map symbols (for example, tourist information centre/campsite/train station) so that you spend less time on any mapwork question and have more time for the more valuable second layer questions.

3. Weather and Climate

(a) Explain the difference between weather and climate.

....
....
.... (2)

(b) Look carefully at the graph below which shows climate data for London.

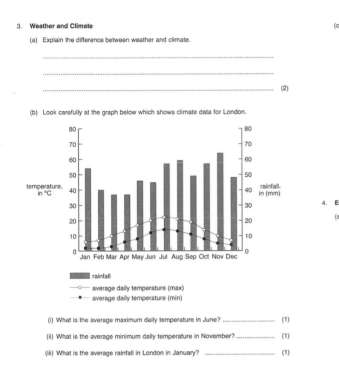

rainfall
average daily temperature (max)
average daily temperature (min)

(i) What is the average maximum daily temperature in June? .... (1)

(ii) What is the average minimum daily temperature in November?.................... (1)

(iii) What is the average rainfall in London in January? .... (1)

(c) (i) Complete the sentence below with the appropriate word.

The British Isles receives three types of rainfall: relief rainfall, convectional rainfall and .... rainfall. (1)

(ii) Some areas of Britain have more rainfall than others. Explain why this is.

....
....
....
....
.... (4)

4. Economic Activity

(a) Sort the following jobs into the correct type of economic activity. *(One has been done for you.)* (2)

| doctor | miner | farmer |
| car plant worker | | shop assistant |

primary	secondary	tertiary
		doctor

■ **Figure 6.2:** Section C layered question

Exam tip

Look at how marks are allocated in your practice papers. This should help you identify the skills and knowledge that you need to practise and revise for the exam. Stay calm if you seem to be taking a while to complete mapwork questions only worth 1 or 2 marks; don't get stuck in a rut. If you are having real trouble with a certain question or skill, move on and come back to it at the end of the paper.

Data sources and drawing diagrams

Often a source of data accompanies a question. This could be a map, a photograph, a table, a graph or a diagram. If this is the case, examine the data carefully before trying to answer the question. If there are figures available, use them to support your answer. For example, there may be a map of Britain showing temperature differences between different regions. The question may ask you to give an explanation for these differences. In your answer you should, of course, give an explanation, but also refer to figures on the map.

Other questions require you to draw diagrams. You may be asked, for example, to explain how the processes of freeze-thaw weathering occur or how a waterfall on a river is formed. In this case you will either be given a large box in which to draw your diagrams, or a smaller box with lines below for you to write an explanation of what you have drawn in the box. In both cases, but particularly when there is nowhere for a written explanation, it is vital that you add detailed labels to explain the processes occurring. A series of small diagrams can often explain the stages of a process more clearly than one big diagram.

> **→ Exam tip**
>
> Location knowledge questions often demand that you name or plot location knowledge information using an outline map provided with the paper. When plotting information on an outline map be sure to be accurate and clear to avoid losing marks. Always use pencil in case you have misinterpreted the question and need to rub out your answer.

Longer answer questions – syllabus example questions based on specific aspects of the topics you have studied

Question focus and format

The final layer of a question may carry the highest number of marks and will often ask you about a syllabus example (case study) you have studied in class. There are case studies for the following topics: Earthquakes and Volcanoes, Rivers and Coasts, Population and Settlement and Transport and Industry.

If you have used both *Geography for Common Entrance* textbooks while studying for Geography CE you will be well prepared to answer any section C question. Each book contains case studies that can be discussed in this section of the exam. All case studies within these books begin with an explanation of the theory concerning the case study, followed by a factual explanation of what happened, often analysing the consequences within the categories of immediate and then long-term effects.

Common mistakes

Ordnance Survey mapwork

Four and six figure grid references
You should have learnt the rules that apply to this skill in class but under pressure it is easy to forget that you always read or use the easting (bottom) figure first then the northing (side) figure last. As with all skills, practice makes perfect and eliminates mistakes.

Accuracy
Giving a rough or inaccurate answer could lose you some or all of the marks in a mapwork question that asks you, for example, to measure the distance along a road using the scale, or to measure the height increase up a slope using contour lines. A few seconds checking your answer and making sure it is correct could get you the vital marks you need. Taking string into the exam will mean measuring windy routes is quick and easy. Simply lay the string along the route and then straighten it out to measure it, referring to the scale on the map.

Shorter and longer answer questions

Technical terms
During your classes in the years leading up to the Common Entrance Geography exam, you will have come across many of the technical terms that will be used in the exam questions. If you do not understand the meaning of a word or words in a question, you will not be able to answer it, even if you know everything about that topic. How frustrating! For example here is a question used in a previous paper.

'Look at the OS extract. Describe the ways in which *conflicting economic demands* may have affected the *environment* shown on the map.'

You may understand how the wildlife and local people can be affected by the growth of different industries (which is what the question is asking) but you may not understand one or more of the words in italics, preventing you from answering the question well, if at all. Both *Geography for Common Entrance* textbooks highlight such key terms within the text and explain their meaning in the glossary at the end of the book. To help you further, study the command words that examiners use in the exam questions (pages 154–155).

> **→ Exam tip**
> As well as learning the meaning of key terms so that you can understand the question, it is also a good idea to use these terms in your answers to get the highest mark possible.

Identifying your mistakes

The mistakes mentioned so far happen often and are made, to some degree, by all students. However, your teacher will probably give you plenty of past examination paper questions as practice questions, and you will complete one or two mock exam papers before doing the real thing in the summer. It is a really good idea to keep all these practice questions and papers and look through them when revising to see if you can identify any of the mistakes discussed above, or any mistake that you have made more than once. Learn from your mistakes and improve your exam technique.

Location knowledge

The few mistakes that are made with these questions are a result of rushing and inaccuracy, as they are at the end of the paper and time is all too often running out. The best way to avoid mistakes is simply to learn everything you need to know (remember that location knowledge is covered in both *Geography for Common Entrance* textbooks). When you are asked to plot a city, desert, mountain range or similar on the map it is important to plot it clearly and accurately. The advice is simple: learn it!

Reading exam questions

Here is some general advice that applies to all parts of the paper. It is advice you have heard before and will hear again, and there is a reason for this! It is absolutely essential that you read the instructions on the front of the paper, know what to do and how long you have to do it. The exam in its present form is one hour long and you have to answer all the questions. Always read the question carefully, twice to be sure, especially where it is worth several marks. Just as important is to make sure you do answer the question. Look for key words or terms in the question to identify what it wants from you.

Examples of strong and weak answers

To help you produce good answers to questions we will now illustrate what constitutes a strong and a weak answer to the same question using two past paper questions. The shorter answer example question is based on the topic of tectonic processes and refers to a world map showing how the world is split up into tectonic plates. The longer answer example question refers to the OS map in that particular paper which was centred on a National Park. For both questions we have given a strong answer and explained why it is good, plus a weak answer and explained why it is poor. Notice the differences between the quality of the strong and weak answers. Look at past papers or test questions you have done, then identify which answers are strong and which are weak.

Shorter answer example question

Explain why the distribution of earthquakes and volcanoes are so similar. Use the information from the map to support your answer. (5 marks – 8 lines)

Strong answer

Earthquakes and volcanoes both occur on plate boundaries. There are four different types of plate boundary. A constructive boundary where plates move apart such as the American and Eurasian plates which create new islands like Sertsey near Iceland shown on the map. Destructive plate boundaries where oceanic plates go under continental, creating earthquakes and volcanoes such as the Andes mountains. Conservative boundaries, such as the San Andreas fault, USA shown on the map, where two plates slide past each other causing earthquakes. Finally collision boundaries where two continental plates push together creating mountain ranges such as the Himalayas.

Why it is a strong answer

- It immediately answers the question – *earthquakes and volcanoes both occur on plate boundaries.*
- It goes further to show the candidate's understanding of the different types of plate boundaries.
- It seeks extra marks by referring to specific examples.
- It refers to the data source (the world map showing how the world is split into tectonic plates) on at least two occasions, as suggested in the question.

Weak answer

Earthquakes happen on plates and are spread across the world. In America there was a big earthquake that killed lots of people and they now make special buildings that are earthquake proof.

Why it is a weak answer

- It does not answer the question. The pupil needed to say that earthquakes and volcanoes occur at specific places which are called plate boundaries. They are not spread evenly across the world.
- It only talks about earthquakes when the question asked about the distribution of earthquakes and volcanoes.
- It vaguely discusses an example but this is an irrelevant one that is lacking any statistics to back it up.
- At no point does it refer to the map as suggested in the question.
- It does not use the eight lines available on the paper for the answer.

With reference to examples you have studied, describe the ways in which tourists affect the natural environment of scenic areas, such as the one on the map, and explain what has been done to address these problems. (8 marks – 18 lines)

Strong answer

Tourists have damaged the environment in the Peak District National Park in many ways. Over 17 million people live within 60 miles of the Park concentrated in large urban areas such as Manchester, Nottingham and Sheffield with good access to the Park (M1/M6). This means most visitors arrive by car which causes high levels of air pollution as well as causing traffic congestion, both of which are significantly worse in the summer when over 10 000 cars per day use the Park's narrow roads. The activities tourists come to enjoy can also cause damage to the landscape and wildlife creating conflict with the farmers who own most of the land. Walkers often cause soil erosion by not keeping to footpaths, leave farmers' gates open or damage their walls by scrambling over them. More energetic activities such as hang-gliding and mountain biking can frighten wildlife or farmers' livestock and damage delicate vegetation which forms the habitat for species of wild birds.

In an attempt to reduce the levels of pollution and congestion created by visitors arriving by car, the Peak District National Park Authority have introduced park and ride schemes which allow tourists to arrive on the borders of the Park by car but then use public transport within the Park. To reduce the conflict that occurs between tourists and farmers the National Park Authority have clearly marked footpaths with signposts, provided separate mountain biking trails to prevent further soil erosion and created specially designated areas for hang-gliding.

Why it is a strong answer
- It immediately introduces an example, as is asked for in the question, to base the rest of the answer upon.
- It gives details of not just one but several ways in which tourists affect the natural environment, referring to specific facts learnt from a case study.
- It goes on to discuss how visitors create conflict not only with the needs of the wildlife in the National Park but also with the interests of local people, in this case farmers.
- It clearly answers the second part of the question which seeks solutions to the problems created by tourism by identifying specific ways in which the National Park Authority have dealt with the problems identified earlier in the question.

Weak answer

Tourism is bad because people litter everywhere and that harms animals which people want to come and see in the first place. I don't think that people should be allowed to drop litter and should be fined if they do in a National Park.

Why it is a weak answer
- It does not use facts and figures from a specific example or examples, as required in the question.
- It only talks about one way in which tourists affect the environment which limits marks.
- It gives a personal opinion in the first person (*I don't think that people should be allowed to drop litter...*) about a solution to problems facing the environment, which is not what the question is asking for.
- It fails to use the eighteen lines available to answer this question.

6.2 The Common Academic Scholarship Examination

The structure of the exam

The CASE paper requires candidates to answer two questions in 60 minutes; one from a choice of two in Section A and one from a choice of around six in Section B. There are five thematic topics within the Geography syllabus, all of which could be tested in the exam. These topics are listed below, along with the *Geography for Common Entrance* textbook in which each topic is covered.

Section A: Data-response questions (25 marks)

Question 1 — *Physical and environmental topics*

Theme	Geography for Common Entrance
Rivers and coasts	Physical Geography
Weather and climate	Physical Geography
Earthquakes and volcanoes	Physical Geography

Question 2 — *Human topics*

Theme	Geography for Common Entrance
Population and settlement	Human Geography
Transport and industry	Human Geography
Environmental issues*	Human Geography

*Note that 'environmental issues' is not a separate topic in the new ISEB Geography syllabus but underpins the topics of Population and settlement and Transport and industry.

Section B: Essay and structured essay questions (25 marks)

Questions based on any of the physical, environmental and human topics covered in Section A, but the thematic topic focus of the two Section A questions is unlikely to be repeated in any of the Section B questions. Fieldwork investigations may also form the question focus of one of the Section B questions. Fieldwork projects do not directly count towards the CASE mark.

Section A questions – data-response questions
Question focus and format

As you can see from the information on page 149, this section of the paper carries half of the marks and demands knowledge from all the thematic topics in the CASE syllabus. Question 1 will be based on a physical or environmental topic and question 2 will be based on a human topic. Both questions however are of a data-response style meaning you will have to analyse, interpret and discuss one or more pieces of information provided with the question. This could be a map, a photograph, a table, a graph or a diagram. Examine the data carefully before trying to answer the question and see if you can express your knowledge within all parts of the question by drawing information from the data to illustrate your answer.

Section A questions are layered into three or four parts with more marks being awarded to the latter parts of the question (see Figure 6.3 on page 151). You can see the pattern of marks in this question which roughly indicates how much you should write and how long you should spend on each part of the question. Parts (a) and (b) of this question must be answered using the candidate's knowledge of the subject but need to refer to the information in the data sources, particularly to the facts that make up resource A. The next layer of the question, part (c), does not necessarily demand candidates refer to the data sources but goes on to offer considerably more marks for a higher level explanation of a hazard that you will have studied within the six thematic topics of the syllabus.

> **Exam tip**
>
> Look at how marks are allocated in Section A of your practice papers. This should help you to identify what you need to include in different parts of Section A questions and subsequently what you need to revise before you take the exam.

SECTION A

Answer EITHER Question 1 OR Question 2.

1. Look at **Resource A** and **Resource B** and then answer the questions.

Resource A

Tornadoes
Worst season for 15 years in US. Over 100 people were killed in events in Tennessee (Nashville) and Alabama. Meanwhile, a small tornado struck Selsey, W. Sussex in the UK.

Freak Weather Hits N and S America.
New York suffers from massive snowfalls. Drought and fires sweep across Brazil, and in Texas, temperatures hit 45 °C for a record 29 consecutive days.

Flooding in Europe
In the UK, large areas of the Midlands and S. Wales were flooded over Easter. Worst hit were Northampton where 1500 homes were affected, Stratford and Shrewsbury. Heavy rains and mudslides were responsible for large numbers of deaths in the Black Tides' disasters in G. Italy.

Flooding in Bangladesh
Over two-thirds of the population were affected by the worst floods of the century, which lasted for over 3 months.

Tectonic Hazards
Earthquakes caused 4000 deaths in Afghanistan, but the most devastating tectonic event occurred in Papua New Guinea where one of the world's largest tsunamis claimed numerous deaths.

Hurricanes
Hurricane Bonnie caused significant damage in the USA. Hurricane Mitch is being called the worst of the century. Much of Central America was hit by this hurricane which claimed 10 000 deaths in Nicaragua. The long-term social and economic impacts may yet prove to be more devastating. Current figures suggest over 20 000 people are dead or missing, 1 million homes were lost and 3 million people lost their livelihood.

Flooding in China
A state of emergency was declared by the Chinese authorities as 400 million people were threatened in the Yangtze basin. Over 1000 people were killed and millions made homeless.

Resource B

River flood damage – a common natural hazard which may require a response from the relevant authorities

(a) **Resource A** shows some of the hazardous events which occurred in one single year in the late 1990s. Why is it so hard to predict these types of hazards and their impact? (6)

(b) Look at **Resource B** and its caption. Why do people live in areas which are frequently flooded? (9)

(c) For a case study of a hazard you have studied, explain the causes of the hazard and the effects it had on the people and the environment. (10)

S.A. 288SC19   2   S.A. 288SC19   3   **Turn over**

■ **Figure 6.3:** Section A layered question

Section B questions – essay and structured essay questions
Question focus and format

As you can see from the information on page 150, this section of the paper also carries half the marks available. There will be around six questions in Section B based on all six thematic topics in the CASE syllabus, as well as the possibility of a question based on fieldwork investigations candidates may have carried out in the years leading up to the exam. As well as a range of questions based on differing thematic topics to choose from, candidates will also be presented with two different styles of questions.

Structured essay questions are similar in format to those in Section A in that they may have three of four parts that relate to each other. However, the mark value for each part can vary significantly so do not be fooled into thinking you will do well on this type of question unless you have looked at each part of the question carefully and decided how you will answer it and whether you can provide enough information to justify the mark value of that part. Look at Figure 6.4 on page 152 which is an example of this sort of structured essay question. Notice that part (b) is worth twice as many marks as parts (a) and (c). You should always plan your answers to this type of question before you begin, giving particular attention in your plan to the part worth most marks.

6. The development of tertiary and quaternary activities within a country suggests an advanced economy.

(a) Explain what is meant by this statement. (6)

(b) Using an economic activity you have studied, describe the reasons for its location and the changes which have taken place in recent years. (12)

(c) Has the growth of your economic activity been helpful or not to the growth of other economic activities in the area studied? (7)

■ **Figure 6.4:** Section B structured essay question

Essay questions are not divided into parts but simply pose one question to which candidates need to write an essay-style answer that will be marked out of 25 (Figure 6.5 below).

4. The environment has become one of the key political issues of our time. What can the study of geography contribute to this debate? (25)

■ **Figure 6.5:** Section B essay-style question

It is essential that you plan essay answers to avoid losing focus, repeating information and panicking as time starts to run out at the end of the exam. Answers should always relate to the theory that underpins the topic focus and should discuss case studies you have studied. To get the highest marks in this type of question you should attempt, if the question permits, to create an argument and bring into the essay aspects of other thematic topics you have studied. You should ask yourself the following questions before attempting an essay question and keep in mind your answers to these questions when you plan how to answer the question:

● Are the points I am going to make answering the question?

● Do I have plenty of facts and figures relating to at least one case study to back up my answer?

● Am I going to show the examiner my understanding of the theory of the topic on which the question is based?

● Am I going to create an argument within my answer and explain different sides of the argument?

● Am I able to link my answer to this question with other thematic topics?

> **Exam tip**
>
> Do not choose to do a question in Section B because you prefer the particular style of that question. The most important factor in deciding which question to choose in this section is how well you can answer the question and how well you can express to the examiner your understanding and knowledge of the thematic topic upon which the question is based.

Common mistakes

Timing

Strangely enough, knowing too much information can sometimes be a problem because you simply do not have time to put it down on paper in the exam! You need to learn to be concise, precise and 'mark targeted' when answering any question on the CASE paper to avoid mismanaging your time. This skill comes with practice. It is particularly easy to spend too long answering the question you have chosen in Section A which will then cause you to be under time pressure when choosing and writing your answer in Section B. So, keep a close eye on your watch throughout the exam and plan your time as well as what you are going to write.

Essay-style errors

CASE examiners are looking for evidence that the candidate whose paper they are marking has an excellent understanding of Geography. To help show you are such a candidate it is always useful to use the correct geographical terms within a topic.

Both Galore Park Geography textbooks highlight such key terms within the text and explain their meaning in the glossary at the end of each chapter. To help you further, at the end of this chapter you can study the command words Geography CASE examiners use in the exam questions (pages 154–155).

When discussing your own opinions within an answer try to avoid using the first person all the time (for example, I think ...). Here are some alternative starting points to use as a tool for expressing your own opinion within an answer:

- It is believed ...
- A solution would be ...
- One suggests ...
- A common view of this ...
- This problem could be overcome by ...

Repeating information

If you do not read thoroughly and analyse what each part of a layered question is asking, and you do not plan how you are going to respond to each part of the question, it is very easy to find yourself repeating similar or the same information in different parts of the same question. Obviously an examiner cannot give you marks for the same points or information more than once in the exam, so avoid this costly error by quickly planning all parts of all questions before you attempt them.

Identifying your mistakes

The mistakes mentioned so far happen often and are made, to some degree, by all students. However, your teacher will probably give you plenty of past CASE paper questions as practice questions, and you will complete one or two mock CASE papers before doing the real thing in the summer. It is a really good idea to keep all these practice questions and papers and look through them when revising to see if you can identify any of the mistakes discussed above, or any mistake that you have made more than once. Learn from your mistakes and improve your exam technique.

Reading exam questions

Here is some general advice that applies to all parts of the paper. It is advice you have heard before and will hear again, and there is a reason for this! It is absolutely essential that you read the instructions on the front of the paper, know what to do and how long you have to do it. The exam in its present form is one hour long and you have to answer one question from a choice of two in Section A and one question out of a choice of around six questions in Section B. Always read the question carefully, twice to be sure, especially where it is worth several marks. Just as important is to make sure you do answer the question. Look for key words or terms in the question to identify what it wants from you and avoid repeating the same information in different parts of the same question.

Syllabus command words

Note and understand the following command words used in Common Entrance and Common Academic Scholarship papers:

annotate	add descriptive explanatory labels
choose	select carefully from a number of alternatives
complete	finish, make whole
define	give an exact description of
describe	write down the nature of the feature
develop	expand upon an idea
explain	write in detail how something has come into being and/or changed
give	show evidence of
identify	find evidence of
list	put a number of examples in sequence

mark and name	show the exact location of and add the name
name	give a precise example of
select	pick out as most suitable or best
shade and name	fill in the area of a feature and add the name
state	express fully and clearly in words
study	look at and/or read carefully
suggest	propose reasons or ideas for something

Note and understand the following command words used in Common Academic Scholarship papers only:

discuss	present viewpoints from various aspects of a subject
elaborate	similar to *expand* and *illustrate*
expand	develop an argument and/or present greater detail on
illustrate	use examples to develop an argument or a theme

Good luck!

Appendix: Ordnance Survey map keys

Key taken from 1:25 000 scale OS Explorer maps

Ordnance Survey®

Explorer™ series (1:25 000 scale)

ROADS AND PATHS   Not necessarily rights of way

M1 or A6(M)	Motorway Ⓢ Service Area ⁊ Junction
A 35	Dual carriageway
A 31(T) or A35	Trunk or Main road
B 3074	Secondary road
	Narrow road with passing places
	Road under construction
	Road generally more than 4 m wide
	Road generally less than 4 m wide
	Other road, drive or track, fenced and unfenced
	Gradient: steeper than 20% (1 in 5)
	14% (1 in 7) to 20% (1 in 5)
Ferry	(V) Vehicle; (P) Passenger
	Path

RAILWAYS

	Multiple track } Standard
	Single track } gauge
	Narrow gauge / Light Rapid Transit System
	Road over; road under; level crossing
	Cutting; tunnel; embankment
	Station, open to passengers; siding

PUBLIC RIGHTS OF WAY   Not shown on maps of Scotland

....	Footpath
– – – –	Bridleway
+–+–+–+	Byway open to all traffic
–·–·–·–	Road used as a public path

The representation on this map of any other road, track or path is no evidence of the existence of a right of way

OTHER PUBLIC ACCESS

• • •   Other routes with public access

The exact nature of the rights on these routes and the existence of any restrictions may be checked with the local highway authority. Alignments are based on the best information available.

◆ ◆	National Trail / Long Distance Route; Recreational route
....	Permitted footpath }
– – – –	Permitted bridleway } See note below

Footpaths and bridleways along which landowners have permitted public use but which are not rights of way. The agreement may be withdrawn.

• • •   Off road cycle routes

BOUNDARIES

—+—+—	National
—·—·—	County
– – – –	Constituency (Const), Electoral Region (ER) or Burgh Const
....	Civil Parish (CP) or Community (C)
– – – –	Unitary Authority (UA),
	National Park or Forest Park boundary

GENERAL FEATURES

Gravel pit		△	Triangulation pillar
Sand pit		⊺	Mast
Other pit or quarry		⚥	Windmill; with or without sails
Landfill site or slag heap		⚥ ⚥	Wind pump; wind generator
Place of worship	with tower	pylon pole	Electricity transmission line
	with spire, minaret or dome	⁙⁙⁙⁙⁙	Slopes
	without such additions	BP	Boundary post
Building; important building		BS	Boundary stone
Glasshouse		CH	Clubhouse
Youth hostel		FB	Footbridge
Bunkhouse/camping barn/		MP; MS	Milepost; milestone
		PO	Post office
Bus or coach station		Pol Sta	Police station } selected areas only
Lighthouse; disused lighthouse;		Sch	School }
Beacon		TH	Town Hall
		NTL	Normal tidal limit
		· W; Spr	Well; spring

HEIGHTS AND NATURAL FEATURES

52 ·   Ground survey height
284 ·   Air survey height

Surface heights are to the nearest metre above mean sea level. Heights shown close to a triangulation pillar refer to the ground level height at the pillar and not necessarily at the summit

Vertical face/cliff

				75
				60
				50
Loose rock	Boulders	Outcrop	Scree	

Water			Mud

Sand; sand and shingle

ACCESS LAND

Land open to the public by permission of the owners. The agreement may be withdrawn.

National Trust, always open; limited access - observe local signs

National Trust for Scotland, always open; limited access - observe local signs

Woodland Trust

Forestry Commission

AL   Other Access Land

►   Access Information Point

▼ DANGER AREA ◄ ►
▲

Firing and test ranges in the area.
Danger!
Observe warning notices

VEGETATION

Vegetation limits are defined by positioning of symbols

	Coniferous trees
	Non-coniferous trees
	Coppice
	Orchard
	Scrub
	Bracken, heath or rough grassland
	Marsh, reeds or saltings.

ARCHAEOLOGICAL AND HISTORICAL INFORMATION

✝	Site of antiquity
⚔ 1066	Site of battle (with date)
VILLA	Roman
𝕮𝖆𝖘𝖙𝖑𝖊	Non-Roman
✶ ⁙⁙⁙	Visible earthwork

Key taken from 1:25 000 scale OS Explorer maps (continued)

Ordnance Survey®

Explorer™ series (1:25 000 scale)

TOURIST AND LEISURE INFORMATION

Building of historic interest	Other tourist feature
Cadw: Welsh Historic Monuments	Parking
Camp site / Caravan site	Park and ride (all year / seasonal)
Camping and caravan site	Picnic site
Castle, Fort	Preserved railway
Cathedral, Abbey	PC Public Convenience
Country park	Public house/s
Cycle trail	Recreation / Leisure / Sports centre
English Heritage	Slipway
Fishing	Telephone (public / motoring organisation)
Garden/Arboretum	Theme/Pleasure park
Golf course or links	Viewpoint
Historic Scotland	Visitor centre
Information centre (all year / seasonal)	Walks/Trails
Horse riding	Water activites
Museum	
Nature reserve	

Scale 1: 25 000

4 centimetres to 1 kilometre (one grid square)

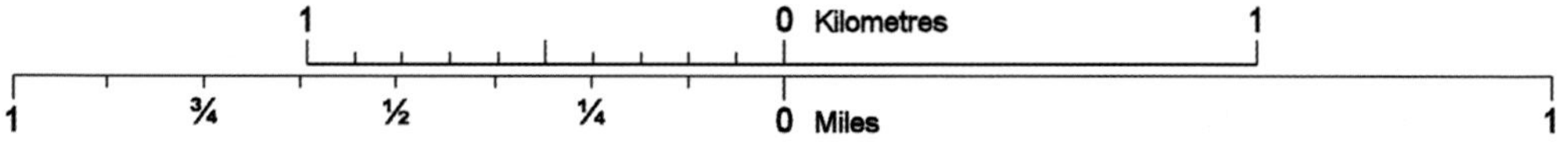

1
0 Kilometres
1
1
¾
½
¼
0 Miles
1

NB. Due to changes in specification there are differences on some sheets

Made, printed and published by Ordnance Survey, Southampton, United Kingdom. **For educational use only.**

Ordnance Survey®

OS Landranger® (1:50 000 scale)

ROADS AND PATHS
Not necessarily rights of way

	Motorway (dual carriageway)
	Motorway under construction
	Primary Route
	Main road
	Primary Route / Main road under construction
	Secondary road
	Narrow road with passing places
	Road generally more than 4m wide
	Road generally less than 4m wide
	Path / Other road, drive or track
	Gradient: 20% (1 in 5) and steeper,
	Gates / Road Tunnel
	Ferry (passenger) / Ferry (vehicle)

Service area (S)
Junction number [1]
Elevated
M1
Unfenced   Footbridge
A 470   Dual carriageway
A 493
B 4518
A 855   Bridge   B 885
Ferry P   Ferry V

RAILWAYS

Track multiple or single	Bridges / Footbridge
Track under construction	Level crossing / LC
Siding	Viaduct
Tunnel	Station, (a) principal
Light rapid transit system,	Light rapid transit system

WATER FEATURES

Marsh or salting
Slopes   Cliff
Towpath   Lock   Shingle
Aqueduct   Canal   Ford   Beacon   Flat rock   Lighthouse (in use)
    Sand   Lighthouse (disused)
Weir   Normal tidal limit   Dunes   Low water mark
Lake   Footbridge   Bridge   Mud
    High water mark
Canal (dry)

HEIGHTS

1 metre = 3·2808 feet

50	Contours are at 10 metres
·144	Heights are to the nearest

Heights shown close to a triangulation pillar

ROCK FEATURES

Outcrop   650
Cliff   600
Scree

LAND FEATURES

	Electricity transmission line
	Pipe line
ruin	Buildings
	Public building (selected)
	Bus or coach station
	Place of worship — with tower / with spire, minaret or dome / without such additions
o	Chimney or tower
	Glass structure
(H)	Heliport
△	Triangulation pillar
	Mast
	Wind pump / wind generator
	Windmill with or without sails
+	Graticule intersection at 5' intervals
	Cutting / embankment
	Quarry
	Spoil heap, refuse tip or dump
	Coniferous wood
	Non-coniferous wood
	Mixed wood
	Orchard / Park or ornamental ground
	Forestry Commission
	National Trust-always open
	National Trust-limited access, observe local signs
	National Trust for Scotland

◯ Key taken from 1:50 000 scale OS Landranger maps (continued)

OS **Ordnance Survey®**

OS Landranger® (1:50 000 scale)

PUBLIC RIGHTS OF WAY

----------------- Footpath
- - - - - - - - Bridleway
-·-·-·-·-·-·- Road used as a public path
-+-+-+-+-+-+ Byway open to all traffic

The symbols show the defined route so far as the scale of mapping will allow. Rights of way are not shown on maps of Scotland.

The representation on this map of any other

Danger Area   Firing and Test Ranges in

BOUNDARIES

+ — + — + — + National
-+- -+- -+- -+- District
—·—·—·—·— County, Unitary Authority,

National Park

OTHER PUBLIC ACCESS

• • • • Other route with public access

◆ ◆ National Trail, European Long

● ● National/Regional Cycle Network
— — Surfaced cycle route
4 8 National/Regional Cycle Network

ANTIQUITIES

+ Site of monument
· ○ Stone monument
⚔ Battlefield (with date)
☆ ···· Visible earthwork
VILLA Roman
Castle Non-Roman

TOURIST INFORMATION

⋏ Camp site
🚐 Caravan site
✿ Garden
⚑ Golf course or links
i i Information centre, all year / seasonal
⚐ Nature reserve
P P&R Parking, Park and ride, all year / seasonal
⚔ Picnic site
▨ Selected places of tourist interest
✆ ✆ Telephone, public / motoring organisation
⚜ Viewpoint
V Visitor centre
! Walks / Trails
▲ Youth hostel

ABBREVIATIONS

CG	Coastguard	P	Post office
CH	Club house	PC	Town Hall, Guildhall or equivalent
MP	Milepost	PH	Public house
MS	Milestone		

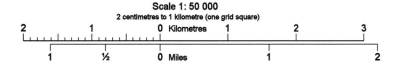

Scale 1: 50 000
2 centimetres to 1 kilometre (one grid square)

2 1 0 Kilometres 1 2 3

1 ½ 0 Miles 1 2

Ordnance Survey, the OS Symbol and OS Landranger are registered trademarks of Ordnance Survey, the national mapping agency of Great Britain.   July 2002
Made, printed and published by Ordnance Survey, Southampton, United Kingdom. **For educational use only.**   © Crown copyright 2002

Glossary

Syllabus words are underlined

Ageing population   An increasing percentage of a country's population reaching middle and old age, placing pressure on healthcare resources.

Agriculture   The practice of farming, including the cultivation of the soil, for the growing of crops and the rearing of animals to provide food, wool and other products.

Aid   Money and resources given to those in need following famine or natural disasters.

Alternative energy   Energy that is made from renewable resources such as solar power, HEP and geothermal energy.

Arable farming   The farming of crops in soil.

Arterial road   An important road that links suburbs of the city with the CBD of the city. Usually an 'A' road and often a dual carriageway.

Assemble   Put parts together to make a product, e.g. cars on an assembly line.

Atmosphere   The mass of gases surrounding the earth, as well as one aspect that helps to describe an environment.

Bearing   Compass direction given in degrees (360° in the complete circle).

Biodegrade   The process of an object being broken down naturally by nature.

Biodiversity   The number and variety of all living things within an ecosystem.

Birth rate   The number of babies born per 1000 in a particular country.

Brownfield site   Disused or derelict urban land which is available for redevelopment.

Business Park   A development of offices and industrial units.

Bypass   A road built around a town to help cut congestion within the town.

Catchment area   The area from which people will travel to a shop or service.

Census   A large survey conducted by the government every ten years which asks everybody in the UK questions about their lives.

Central Business District (CBD)   The centre of a city or town, associated with high rise offices, shops and entertainment facilities.

Commute   To travel to work some distance from where you live.

Comparison goods   Expensive items that people need to compare in price before buying and will travel a long way to buy, such as jewellery, electronic items and clothes.

Compass   An instrument used to identify direction.

Components   Pre-manufactured parts that are put together on an assembly line.

Conflict   A disagreement between two or more people (or groups of people). For example, land use conflict between tourists and farmers in National Parks.

Conservation   The protection, preservation or restoration of the environment.

Containerisation   To transport goods in standard sized, sealed containers.

Contour line   A brown line on a map joining places of the same height together.

Conurbation   Large urban area formed from the merging of towns and villages as population has grown and expansion has taken place.

Convenience goods   Cheap goods that people need on a regular basis and will not travel far to buy, such as newspapers, milk and bread.

Counterurbanisation The process of people moving back to rural areas from the city.

Country Parks Areas of countryside that are protected from development.

Death rate The number of people per 1000 who die in a particular country.

Deforestation The cutting down and clearing of forested areas which often leads to soil erosion and other environmental consequences.

Densely populated Many people living in a particular area.

Desertification The process by which areas of desert are created by the destruction of natural vegetation.

Detached housing Housing that is within its own grounds, often found in the outer suburbs.

Development How rich or poor a country is in comparison with other countries. Measured by indicators such as GNP, health standards, life expectancy, etc.

Dispersed settlement Individual houses or small groups of houses spread thinly across a given area, often found in agricultural or mountainous areas.

Distribution The spread of an activity across a given area, e.g. farming types across Britain.

Diversification The process of farmers using their land for activities other than farming, encouraged by government schemes such as set-aside.

Dormitory settlement A village that has expanded due to a large proportion of its population commuting to larger settlements.

Drought A prolonged period of below average precipitation.

Easting A vertical blue grid line on an OS map.

Economy The state of a country or region in terms of the production and consumption of goods and services and the supply of money.

Ecosystem An area displaying a distinctive interaction between plants, animals and the physical environment.

Eco-tourism Low impact tourism aimed at protecting the natural environment and local cultures.

Emigration The process of people moving abroad permanently.

Employment The state of having paid work.

Endangered species Animals, insects or plants which are at risk of becoming extinct.

Environment The physical setting where humans, plants and animals live amongst each other (the landscape, the atmosphere and the habitat).

Environment Agency Government department charged with protecting the environment.

Ethnic group People of the same cultural background.

European Union (EU) A group of 28 (as at 1st July 2013) European countries which have grouped together to make trade and aid easier for each other.

Exploit To use a situation seen as beneficial to some people in a way that is unfair to other people; to seek and to use a natural resource for human benefit.

Extensive farming The operation of farms that do not spend a lot of money on machinery and labour and are usually on a large scale e.g. sheep farms.

Fallow   Fields allowed to return to grass instead of being ploughed for growing crops.

Fertile   A term used to describe a soil that has many nutrients and therefore is very good for growing crops on, often found on the floodplains of rivers benefiting from alluvium deposits (silt).

Floodplain   The flat land either side of a river in lowland that is very good for farming.

Footloose   Industries that can locate in a variety of locations and are not tied down to one place by heavy or perishable raw materials.

Forced migration   The movement of people against their will.

Fossil fuels   Non-renewable power resources, for example: coal, oil and natural gas.

Four-figure grid reference   A set of two, two-digit numbers indicating the grid square in which an object is located on an OS map.

Freight   The transport of raw materials and goods by ship, train, lorry or other similar means of transport.

Function   The purpose or purposes of a settlement, which change and often increase in number over time.

GDP   Gross Domestic Product is one of the ways of measuring the size of a country's economy. The GDP of a country is defined as the total value of all goods and services produced within the country in a given period of time (usually a calendar year).

Geothermal energy   Heat and electricity produced from hot, underground water.

Globalisation   The process of spreading company ideas and business around the world.

Global warming   Rapid heating of the earth's atmosphere caused by the build-up of greenhouse gases such as carbon dioxide.

GNP   Gross National Product is the GDP of a country plus the income earned from foreign investments. (See GDP.)

Gradient   Term used to describe the steepness of a slope.

Grant   Money given by the government, e.g. to farmers, to promote production of a particular form of agricultural product such as milk.

Green belt   A band of countryside surrounding a city in which urban growth is regulated to prevent the city spreading.

Green energy   Renewable sources of energy such as solar, wind and HEP.

Greenfield site   Land that has not been built on before, often used for agriculture.

Grid squares   The area of 1 kilometre square created by the grid lines on an OS map.

Habitat   The natural environment of plants and animals.

HDI   Human Development Index is a measure which combines indicators of life expectancy, literacy, education and income for countries worldwide.

HEP   Hydroelectric power – energy created by harnessing the power of fast moving water from a dam using turbines.

Hierarchy   A chart (often a pyramid) ranking settlements by their size and the number of services they have.

High order service   Shops selling comparison (high order) goods. High order goods cost a lot but are not bought very often, such as electronic items.

Hi-tech goods   Lightweight telecommunications and computer equipment such as mobile phones and laptop computers.

Honeypot site   A town, village or attraction in a National Park which is very popular with tourists.

HS2   High Speed Railway 2 – a planned high-speed railway proposed to run between London (Euston), the Midlands and the North of England.

Human factors   Those aspects of society, including location of the market and the intervention of government, which affect a farmer's decision about where to locate and the type of farming.

Human features   Man-made features such as schools and churches.

Illegal immigrant   Somebody who has entered another country for work or better living standards without permission.

Immigrant   Somebody who has officially moved permanently to a different country.

Indicators of development   Measures of how developed a country is, such as GNP and HDI.

Industrial Revolution   A period of history when the invention and use of steam-powered machines led to a massive increase in the number of factories. As most factories were located in towns and cities, people left the countryside to work in them. This first began in Britain between the late 18th and early 19th centuries before spreading to the rest of the world.

Industries   Economic activity concerned with the processing of raw materials and the manufacture of goods in factories.

Infrastructure   Basic but essential communications and services such as schools, hospitals, roads, water and electricity supply.

Inner city   Land use zone of the city which has a lot of terraced housing.

Inner suburbs   Land use zone of the city which has a lot of semi-detached housing.

Intensive farming   Farming with the aim of achieving maximum production within a limited area, especially by using chemicals and machines.

International migration   The movement of people to another country to seek work, health and social benefits.

Key   A list of all the symbols used on a map and their meanings.

Labour   People who work.

Labour intensive   Requiring lots of labour (e.g. textile manufacturing).

Landfill   The disposal of waste in natural or man-made holes in the ground.

Landscape   The natural and human features of an area.

Land use   What is built upon a piece of land.

Life expectancy   The average age that men and women may expect to live until in a particular area or country.

Linear settlement   Houses and buildings arranged in a line along a road, river, valley bottom, etc. (See Ribbon settlement.)

Living wage   A wage that will give an employee enough money for food and housing.

Location factor   A reason why an industry may choose to be located in a certain place.

Low order service Shops selling convenience (low order) goods. Low order goods cost less than high order goods but are bought more regularly, such as food.

Malnutrition Adults and children receiving insufficient food leading to disease and ultimately death.

Manufacture To make products such as cars, furniture and electrical items from raw materials.

Market The place/point where goods and services are sold.

Market gardening Growing of fruit and vegetables in controlled greenhouse conditions.

Migration The movement of people from one area to another seeking work, health and social benefits.

Mixed farming The use of a single farm for multiple purposes, e.g. arable and pastoral farming.

Model A simplified view of how cities in general are split into different zones.

Modernised Rebuilt or refurbished.

Monoculture Growing just one crop in a field year after year.

Multi-national corporations Businesses that have offices or factories in several countries.

National grid National network for supplying electricity.

National Park An area of beautiful countryside that has been designated by law to have its natural beauty and heritage conserved and to promote its benefits to the public.

Natural increase A rise in a country's population level due to more people being born than dying.

NIC Newly Industrialised Countries are those countries whose economies are undergoing rapid economic growth, outpacing other developing countries, but that have not yet reached developed country status. NICs include Brazil, Russia, China and India.

Noise pollution Pollution caused by noise from air and car traffic, nightclubs, building sites, quarries etc.

Nomadic Term describing early populations that hunted and gathered food so did not settle in one place.

Non-renewable resource A resource such as coal, oil, natural gas or nuclear power (uranium) that can only be used once and will therefore at some stage run out.

Northing A horizontal blue grid line on an OS map.

Nuclear power Energy produced by nuclear reactors.

Nucleated settlement Buildings and houses that are arranged in a circular manner around a crossroads, castle, market place, etc.

OS Ordnance Survey.

Outer suburbs Land use zone of the city which has a variety of different purposes and is often surrounded by a ring road.

Overpopulation Overstretching of resources such as food and energy caused by rapid population growth.

Package holidays   Holidays that include the flight, hotel or self-catering accommodation and the help of a resort representative.

Pastoral farming   Rearing animals such as sheep or cows.

Perishable goods   Goods that will go bad in a short period of time such as fruit and vegetables.

Pesticides   Chemicals sprayed on crops to kill insects that could damage the crop.

Physical factors   Natural influences such as the weather or relief on the location of an activity such as farming.

Physical features   Natural features such as rivers and hills.

Physical landscape   The natural features of an area such as trees, rivers and mountains.

Plan view   Looking at something as if from above.

Planned settlements   Houses and buildings built from scratch in a well planned ordered form.

Plateau   An elevated area of high land with a relatively flat surface.

Pollution   Contamination of the environment by gases, noise, litter or waste produced by individuals or industry.

Population density   A measurement of population living in a particular area.

Population explosion   The rapid growth in global population levels in the last 300 years, and particularly in the last 50 years.

Poverty gap   The growing difference between the wealthy and very poor people in the world.

Prevailing wind   A wind from the predominant, or most usual, direction. The prevailing wind in Britain is from the south-west, blowing on average seven days out of ten from this direction.

Primary activities   Taking raw materials from the land and the sea. These tend to be very large and old industries such as farming, fishing, mining and forestry.

Primary industry   Taking raw materials from the land and the sea. These tend to be very large and old industries such as farming, fishing, mining and forestry.

Pull factors   Factors that attract migrants to come to an area such as education, medical and social services.

Push factors   Factors that make migrants want to move away from their local area or country such as political fears, war and poor standards of living.

Quaternary activities   Research and development of new ideas and goods in areas such as medicine and computer technology.

Quota   A set amount of produce a farmer may sell, for example in the European Union.

Range   The distance people will travel to a certain shop.

Raw materials   Natural resources taken from the ground or sea which are used to manufacture items or power.

Recycling   Collecting waste materials and making use of them again.

Refugees   People who have been forced to migrate within a country or from one country to another.

Regulation   Rules applied by companies or governments.

Relief   Physical aspects of the land such as height, gradient and shape.

Relief features   Different landforms illustrated by the shape of the contour lines.

Renewable resource   A resource is said to be renewable if it can be used again and again, such as solar power, HEP and geothermal energy. These resources tend to be expensive to set up, but do not pollute the environment as do non-renewable resources.

Retail   The sale of products to the public.

Ribbon settlement   Houses and buildings arranged in a line along a road, river, valley bottom, etc. (See Linear settlement.)

Ridge   A long area of elevated land with a crest.

Routeway   A line of transport e.g. road, rail, sea or air.

Rural   A place that is predominately in the countryside.

Rural-urban migration   People moving from the countryside to the city.

Safari   A guided tour in search of wild animals.

Savannah   Grassland, lying between the equatorial rain forests and the hot desert regions, which forms the habitat for many African animals.

Scale   The ratio difference between real size and actual size on a map.

Scale bar   A ruler which shows real distances on the map, usually found at the bottom of an OS map.

Scale ratio   A ratio which shows how much bigger features on the map are in real life.

Science park   A specially built environment for high-tech industries which typically have links with a local university.

Seasonal jobs   Jobs that are only for a short time (a season) such as picking fruit in the summer on fruit farms or working in a chalet during the ski season, often in mainland Europe, in the winter.

Secondary activities   Industries that manufacture or process the raw material collected in primary industries, such as food processing, car assembly and oil refining.

Secondary industry   Industries that manufacture or process the raw materials collected in primary industries, such as food processing, car assembly and oil refining.

Semi-detached housing   Houses that are joined to another house on one side only, often found in the inner suburbs.

Service industry   A provision for the public, such as shops, financial services, education, police and health services.

Services   Facilities available in a settlement such as shops and cinemas, schools and hospitals.

Settlement   A place where people live.

Settlement pattern   The shape of a settlement (linear/nucleated/dispersed).

Shanty town   A rapidly growing, unplanned collection of self-made houses, often with no running water, electricity or proper sanitation.

Site   The specific location of a settlement originally as a result of physical factors such as proximity to a river, etc.

Site factors   The specific reasons why settlers chose a site, such as water supply or defence.

Situation   The location of a settlement in relation to its surrounding area.

Six-figure grid reference   A set of two three-digit numbers indicating the exact location of an object on an OS map.

Sketch section   An outline of the relief of a landscape based on an approximation of what the contour lines are showing, and annotated to show the main features.

Soil erosion   The removal of soil by wind or water, often initiated by deforestation.

Sparsely populated   Very few people living in an area.

Spot height   A black dot on an OS map with a number giving its height above sea level in metres.

Standard of living   The level of services people living in a country experience, such as health, education, electricity and running water.

Stewardship   The management and caring for a place or area by a charity, private body or government.

Subsistence agriculture   Growing crops or rearing animals for one's own consumption and not for sale to a secondary industry.

Subsistence farming   When a farmer produces just enough food for his family to eat.

Suburb   A band of housing on the edge of a city.

Suburbanised village   A village in which the number of houses has grown due to increased commuting. It therefore has some resemblance to the suburbs of a city.

Sunrise industry   A long-established business sector that is in decline.

Sunset industry   A newly-developed, growing business sector.

Surplus   Spare food created from agricultural overproduction.

Sustainable development   A concept expressing the need for people and governments to manage responsibly the world's resources and environment for future generations.

Sweatshops   Factories in developing countries that pack many workers into a small space, often with little ventilation or fresh water supply.

Technological revolution   Recent period of history which has seen the rapid development of lightweight telecommunications and computer equipment.

Terraced housing   Rows of houses that are joined together, often found in the inner city.

Tertiary activities   Industries that are involved in selling (retailing) such as supermarkets and department stores, as well as all industries providing services such as entertainment, finance, health and education.

Tertiary industry   Industries that are involved in selling (retailing), such as supermarkets and department stores, as well as all industries providing services, such as entertainment, finance, health and education.

Textile industry   The manufacturing of clothes and fabrics.

Threshold   The minimum population of a settlement to support a shop.

Tourism   When people visit and stay for a short while in destinations in the UK and abroad, for reasons including recreation.

Transnational corporation (TNC)   A company that has different parts of its company or company branches in different countries, often exploiting cheap labour in developing countries.

Triangulation pillar   Spot height surrounded by a blue triangle indicating the highest point in that area an OS map.

United Nations The United Nations (UN), with its headquarters in New York, is an international organisation the aims of which are to enourage cooperation in international law, international security, economic development, social progress and human rights issues across the world.

Urban A place that is mainly covered by buildings such as a town or city.

Urban dwellers People living in urban areas.

Urbanisation The increase in percentage of people living in cities.

Urban renewal Improving the buildings and the environment of an urban area.

Urban sprawl The continued outward growth of cities into the surrounding countryside, which is sometimes restricted by the green belt.

Visual pollution Visual pollution is the term given to items such as unsightly buildings, spoil tips or heavy industrial complexes spoiling the beauty of a natural landscape.

Index